DO-IT-YOURSELF
Home Surveying

———

DO-IT-YOURSELF
Home Surveying

A PRACTICAL GUIDE
TO HOUSE INSPECTION
AND THE DETECTION
OF DEFECTS

GEORGE COLLARD

DAVID & CHARLES
Newton Abbot   London

For Pauline and Ronald
In anticipation of their next move

British Library Cataloguing in Publication Data

Collard, George
  DIY home surveying.
  1. Great Britain. Residences. Surveying
  I. Title
  692

ISBN 0–7153–9268–9

Phototypeset by Typesetters (Birmingham) Ltd
and printed in Great Britain
by Butler & Tanner Ltd, Frome and London
for David & Charles Publishers plc
Brunel House, Newton Abbot, Devon

Contents

List of Illustrations

Figures

Photographs

Acknowledgements

To acknowledge all the sources of information used to compile this book would be a difficult task, as it is so diverse in the subjects it embraces and so dependent upon experience of buildings. Basic acknowledgements are due to those responsible for my training as a civil engineer and for my experience in the Royal Engineers, at Durham University, and at the Open University where I was Director of Estates, but I am also conscious of publications which have helped keep me up to date and have provided me with more detailed aspects of some subjects. Those that come readily to mind are *The Guardian*, especially the property and financial pages; *The Independent*; information issued by the Halifax Building Society; the Building Research Establishment's technical publications; *Building* magazine; *Building Trades Journal* (now *Building Today*); and the *New Civil Engineer*.

There are two people I particularly have to thank – my wife Nanette, who has made me write this in clear English and has contributed to the text, and who has been untiring in her efforts at the typewriter; and Bernard Taylor, architect, artist and friend, who has produced the illustrations.

Introduction

Fewer than 10 per cent of house-buyers have full professional surveys carried out on their prospective homes, and
only 15 per cent have a mini-survey carried out, according
to Britain's biggest estate agent. Yet all houses, even new
ones, have defects – some cosmetic, costing a few hundred
pounds to make good, others more serious and costly. The
latest government survey, published in November 1988,
shows that a quarter of all homes require at least £2,200
spending on them, and that many have potentially serious
structural faults which could cost thousands of pounds to
put right. If you think it can't happen to you, think again –
the horror stories are too numerous to discount.

Having inspected hundreds of buildings of every con-
ceivable age and style, from ancient castle to modern semi,
and having supervised the construction, maintenance and
preservation of hundreds more, from hi-tech laboratories to
family homes, I am struck by the huge difference between
the well designed and built, and the badly designed and
built, the latter being at the heart of most of the horror
stories. The one thing they have in common, however, is
neglect – a lack of care, lack of knowledge and lack of
money, all of which have contributed to their deterioration.

Why do the British treat their property so badly? Council
houses are the worst, but private houses are often as bad.
There seems to be an ignorance of design and materials that
is not so evident in other European countries. There is a
desperate need for rigorous house surveys, and house-
holders ought to be encouraged to do much of this work
themselves, or to call in professional help. When it comes
to buying a property, a proper survey is essential.

The cost of a professional survey for a house of average

size and complexity varies between £150 and £500. The survey is usually carried out by a chartered surveyor, which means – in theory at least – that he can be held liable for negligence and sued for damages. Surveyors pay heavy premiums for their 'professional indemnity' insurance and therefore their first thought when writing their report is their own protection from litigation. They will make certain that the report is hedged with disclaimers about possible hidden defects, whether they be under carpets, under floorboards, behind wardrobes, below ground (which includes drains, mains services and foundations), and disclaimers regarding electrical and plumbing services, boilers, decorations and boundaries. Often they will suggest calling in other experts such as structural engineers or woodworm/damp specialists.

Now, for the 10 per cent of house-buyers who rely on this report, or even the 15 per cent who rely on a mini-survey, that's fine as far as it goes – and I would not wish to discourage anyone from having a professional survey, or ever advise against one – however, all the surveyors I know would prefer knowledgeable clients who had carried out their own surveys first and could present their results to them for investigation and comment.

But if you are one of the 75 per cent who have decided against having an independent survey, then read on – you need this book more than anyone. And don't wave an NHBC (Buildmark) certificate and think a survey isn't necessary. You need it more than you know. How else can you claim the insurance cover the certificate offers on *all* defects which occur in the first two years, and structural defects up to ten years?

This book deals first with the present system, shows its limitations and how to get the best value out of a professional inspection/survey. There is advice on how to think logically about the kind of house you need to suit your lifestyle, and how to go about buying and selling, with an emphasis on viewing and preliminary inspections. Selling a house even provides an opportunity to practise survey techniques and at the same time improve the chances of

No foundations? An arch demonstrates its strength in Ambleside

selling quickly. Individual elements of house building are discussed with their likely defects, and finally a detailed description of the sequence and method of survey is given, and the action to be taken afterwards.

I hope this book will also be of value to the professional surveyor – in its breadth if not its depth – but I have written it in terms best suited to the non-professional, enthusiastic house-owner. And for those who think they know nothing about building and are turned off by the sight of rotting wood, then perhaps this will help to change their attitude. Remember that carrying out a survey means being systematic, using your eyes (and nose sometimes), asking questions and seeking the answers. The golden rule is, 'If it looks wrong, it usually is'.

Learn, enjoy the experience – and save money!

1 · The Present System of Surveys

Faults of the system · Types of survey · Legal liability
Can I do my own survey?

FAULTS OF THE SYSTEM

(a) The different kinds of survey are confusing, in-complete, and contain too many limitations and provisions.

(b) The report is expensive and cannot be sold to another buyer if you decide not to proceed.

(c) There are no cast-iron guarantees or insurances against hidden defects.

(d) The land and boundaries are usually neglected, as are the mains services to the property.

(e) You may be able to sue a negligent surveyor or go to arbitration, but you are likely to be the loser, though your interests are now (since April 1989) better pro-tected in law.

In 1988 *The Guardian* reported the case of a couple who had bought a mid-terrace cottage in Wales for £16,500 – but on the day they should have moved in, builders were tearing the place to pieces. The couple thought they had done the right thing by paying £140 for a house-buyer's survey, which had given the house a clean bill of health with only some minor exceptions. However, after com-pleting the purchase, they were horrified to find that the cottage was infested with dry rot – this cost them £5,000 to deal with. At that time they were faced with legal fees of £3,000 if they sued the surveyor, and the risk of losing this as well if they could not prove the surveyor's negligence *in law*.

The couple felt they should make their plight known so that others would realise the danger of accepting a surveyor's report. They were concerned at the failure of the surveyor to pick up the problem, and at the cost and difficulty of seeking redress. Normally it can take up to two or three years to win compensation through the courts, but in this case the surveyor's insurers were at least willing to discuss an out-of-court settlement if another surveyor confirmed their case.

The Guardian also reported the case of a woman in Durham with a problem relating to flooding after heavy rain. The surveyor who had carried out the inspection had seen the water during his survey, but had put it down to a leak in the central heating system. An RICS (Royal Institution of Chartered Surveyors) spokesman brushed off enquiries as follows:

> A surveyor is responsible if negligent in his inspection or report. This one appears to have seen a defect and reported a possible cause. You state he was wrong, but that does not mean he was negligent. The vendor may have deliberately concealed the defect and may have acted fraudulently. To have a claim you must show you have suffered a loss. Check the condition of the house and make sure the electrics are not affected. If the water is doing, or will do, no damage, there may be no problem. One avenue for a claim is that you paid too much for the house, but remember that you say it is common knowledge that these houses suffer this fault. You may be able to dig a small pit below the floor to collect the water and use a small pump to remove it. The alterations may cost a few hundred pounds, but make sure the right pump is used and the wiring done by a professional. If a substantial loss has been suffered you

may be able to sue the vendor, and if you lack financial resources you may qualify for legal aid.

These are extreme cases, but there are many lesser cases that we hear of more frequently, so it is not surprising that housebuyers are asking:

> What is the point of a survey?
>
> Can I sue the surveyor if he misses a fault?
>
> What kinds of survey are there?
>
> What does a survey cover and what does it exclude?
>
> What does it cost?
>
> How can I get value for money?
>
> Can I sell the report if I decide not to buy?
>
> Is a survey necessary at all if the house is new or if a mortgage inspection is carried out?

This chapter tries to answer these questions, to show the deficiencies in the system, and how to use a DIY survey in conjunction with the present schemes as a 'belt and braces' exercise.

> The foolish man built his house on sand. The rain came down and the floods came, and the winds blew and struck the house, and it fell; and great was the fall of it! The sensible man built his house on rock. Rain came down, floods rose, gales blew and hurled themselves against it, and it fell not, for it was founded upon a rock.

If you do not heed the spiritual warning, at least heed the physical one! If a house is not built soundly in the first place, and if it is not kept in good repair, it will fail when put to the test. In the structure of a building, most havoc is wrought by penetration of rain and damp. Alternate wetting, drying and freezing can prove too much for poorly

Durability and performance are the keynotes of good building

Bad design, poor materials and lack of maintenance all contribute to damp and decay

built or maintained roofs, walls and foundations. Ultra-violet light will break down any felt or asphalt roof if it is unprotected. Timber which is too dry and untreated will warp and lose its strength; too wet, and it will encourage wet rot and dry rot. Woodworm will flourish in most softwoods, and in the right conditions deathwatch beetle will attack hardwoods. Unseasoned and untreated timber, very frequently used in the 'sixties and early 'seventies in windows and doors, will rot in just a few years. Insulation in lofts which has blocked the natural ventilation of the roof at the eaves can cause condensation and wreak damage as great as the heaviest gales, but with no insurance to cover it. If the wrong kind of shale or filling is placed under a concrete floor or the foundations, it will cause these to heave like a sponge pudding; and a missing or defective damp-proof course will result in damp walls, unsightly marks and crumbling plaster.

Over four million homes in this country are in need of extensive repairs and yet, despite all the evidence before their eyes, more than 75% of housebuyers do not have a

Asking for trouble? Gutters must be continuous. These faults are usually ignored in a mortgage survey

structural survey carried out. They are content to leave it to the building society, or they rely on their own judgement.

TYPES OF SURVEY

Building societies and banks have finally abandoned their secrecy and pretence over their 'inspection' and do not call it a structural survey any more. It is a report and valuation for mortgage and insurance assessment which is usually done in half an hour and consists of a general look at the property to see that it actually exists as described, and is not in a state of collapse or major disrepair. In actual fact I have seen valuations which are so wide of the mark (more than 50% in one case) that one suspects that some valuers know little about the property market and even less about rebuilding costs, which constitute the basis for insurance. Needless to say, they usually undervalue the property and never inspect it thoroughly. Their report is of little practical use and in some cases can be positively misleading, but the building societies and banks insist upon having it.

At the time of writing the fee for this valuation will vary between £50 and £200 according to the purchase price. For a £50,000 house it will be about £100 inclusive. However, the fee is likely to rise due to the House of Lords ruling on 20th April 1989 that surveyors were responsible when house-buyers lost money as a result of a negligent *mortgage valuation*. In two test cases the Law Lords decided that housebuyers – at least at the cheap end of the market – were entitled to damages against valuers who failed to exercise reasonable skill and care – nor could this liability be excluded by a small-print disclaimer.

In the first case, the purchaser had bought a £17,500 house in 1980 with an Abbey National Building Society mortgage. The society obtained a valuation for its own purposes, and the lady buyer was charged £36 89p. The Abbey National was the first society to allow borrowers to see valuations and duly sent her a copy. When a chimney collapsed, the buyer sued the valuer. In the county court she won £4,300 damages, and the Law Lords upheld the decision, despite a clause in the valuation to the effect that it was not a structural survey.

In the second case, the Law Lords reinstated a £12,000 damages award which had been cancelled by the Court of Appeal. The award had been made to a couple whose two-bedroom house, bought for £9,000 in 1978 with a council mortgage, later proved unsaleable due to subsidence. They had not seen the valuation.

Lord Templeman maintained that valuers were paid, pro-fessional men who knew that 90 per cent of housebuyers relied on mortgage valuations and did not commission their own surveys.

'In these circumstances it is not fair and reasonable for building societies and valuers to agree together to impose on purchasers the risk of loss arising as a result of incom-petence or carelessness on the part of valuers', he said.

A spokesman for the Royal Institution of Chartered Surveyors commented 'The problem is the very low fee charged for a valuation, and the possibly massive liability at the end of it'. As a result, surveyors are likely to charge a higher fee or insist on a more extensive and therefore more expensive survey; alternatively they may persuade the building societies and banks to stop showing valuation reports to borrowers. The saga still has some way to run.

Most building societies offer an alternative report, called the 'Report and Valuation for Home-buyers'. This, or a mini-survey – a modified scheme suggested by the RICS (Royal Institution of Chartered Surveyors) – costs about twice the basic building society report and provides concise details on the state of repair and condition of the property you are intending to buy, together with an opinion of its open market value.

The inspection covers all those parts of the property that are readily visible or accessible, including the roof space – *if* there is easy access via a roof hatch. It will not normally include tests of the electrical, heating or drainage services. Any major defects noted on those parts of the building examined will be listed, with any recommendations for further investigations or courses of action. The report will not list minor defects. It is not a comprehensive inspection but should be sufficient to obtain a general opinion of the parts of the building that can be seen. About 15% of house-buyers opt for this report.

Note the point that it covers only those parts which are readily visible and accessible. No lifting of carpets, no shifting of furniture, no climbing on roofs – and if real structural problems in the walls and foundations are suspected, or other major defects such as timber infestation or in the drainage system, the surveyor will only recommend yet more investigation by structural engineers, timber pest control experts and drainage contractors. The report does not include a dilapidation schedule of minor repairs, electrical tests, heating and plumbing tests.

10% of house-buyers opt for a *full* structural survey; this is a more detailed report based on a more exhaustive investigation and technical examination of the property – it lists the defects and includes an assessment of any remedial works which may need to be undertaken immediately and in the foreseeable future. Note, however, that not all the timbers and structure are examined. Random checks only on accessible parts is still the rule.

Fees for a full structural survey will vary with the age and size of the property, which is why it is essential to meet the surveyor to discuss the scope, and cost, before he carries out the work. Once agreed, your interests should take precedence over everything else that may arise in the course of the inspection and report. It should be possible to have a thorough survey carried out for about £400 on a modest house, and it is sometimes worth every penny, though with the limitations I have described.

New Houses

Why bother to have a structural survey for a new house with an NHBC certificate? Well, this certificate provides certain guarantees, ie one year for boilers, two years for all building faults, and ten years for structural defects. But, but, BUT . . . it is entirely up to you to find these faults, if they exist, and to report them before the particular guarantee periods expire – and how can you do this without a structural survey? So, a new house will need a thorough inspection before two years have elapsed and a structural survey before ten years.

The Independent Professional Survey

If you do elect to have a *full* structural survey you can, of course, leave it to your building society or bank to select a surveyor for you, and you need never come in contact with him. But because a survey is a personal matter and a personal responsibility, you ought to insist on meeting the surveyor first before committing yourself to one particular firm. If you leave it to the building society, or anyone else for that matter, the report is likely to be unsatisfactory. Moreover, the surveyor will feel you don't wish to involve yourself and his allegiance will be inclined towards the▸

building society or bank, instead of to you which is as it ought to be.

Ask your bank manager, solicitor and building society to recommend two or three surveyors, who must be chartered *building* surveyors and not estates surveyors, quantity surveyors or land surveyors. Ring them, or better still go to see them all, and ask if they are interested in carrying out the survey, how much they charge and when they can do it. Choose the one you feel is attuned to you and your needs – this can often be judged by the number of relevant questions asked; the more that are asked, the better he is likely to be.

When you have chosen your surveyor, ask him – or her – to confirm your instructions, and his fee, in writing. Meanwhile, you should carry out your own inspection as described in this book, and write down all the points which come to your notice. Write down anything that puzzles or worries you – for example: What is the funny smell in the bathroom? . . . Can the kitchen be altered? . . . Is the house liable to flood? . . . Can it be extended? . . . Are the boundaries correct? . . . Is the water pressure good enough? Pass your list to your expert and ask him to check the points out for you.

When you receive his report, read it carefully and then ring him and ask him to explain more fully any matters which are not clear or which worry you. He will be far more explicit, since he is free of the legal shackles which cause many reports to appear so emasculated.

The surveyor should ensure that his inspection is carried out so as to avoid damage to contents and to the property. Ideally the dwelling should be unoccupied and empty of furniture and floor coverings, although this is usually not possible. Every surveyor develops his own sequence of inspection to ensure that all relevant parts of the property are examined closely and that their inter-relationship is considered; his system will probably be similar to that described in more detail in Chapter 7.

The Report

The report is the end product of the survey and should serve the following purposes:

To provide a record of the building, its construction and materials, and whether it is sound, dry and weathertight or has major structural defects.

To provide a balanced valuation of the property, taking into account market conditions and the condition of the property.

To advise on the repairs or modifications required to remedy defects; and to describe any further investigations necessary.

The report should be prepared in simple, direct, grammatical English, free of specialist technical expressions unless they are defined. It should differentiate between indisputable fact, firm opinion, and speculation included for guidance or prognosis; and finally, it should include a statement of rebuilding costs for insurance purposes.

LEGAL LIABILITY

Whatever kind of survey you have done, whoever carries it out should have 'Professional Indemnity Insurance' – since in agreeing to carry out the survey, certain legal obligations are incurred, and the basis of a surveyor's liabilities lies in his contract with his client. It is therefore essential that you yourself are his client, and not an intermediary such as a building society or a solicitor. If a surveyor does his work badly it goes without saying that he cannot expect to be paid for it, but usually the client will also wish to claim damages as financial compensation. For instance, if the surveyor failed to carry out his inspection and to present his report within the agreed time and as a result a house at a bargain price was lost, then a claim could properly be made for compensation. If he is negligent, and as a result you pay more for the property than it is worth, then again you can claim damages for the difference and any consequential costs and inconvenience.

If you only discover the negligence years later, you can still claim, but there is a time limit. The law is very unclear on what this time limit is – it used to be six years, but some would hold that there is now no limit to the liability.

Bill and Audrey Clark bought a house for £50,000, and within a few months discovered that most of the window frames were infested with wet rot and required replacing. They claimed the cost of replacement (£4,500) from the surveyor, but he denied the claim on the grounds that it was a 'hidden defect' which he could not reasonably have been expected to uncover. The Clarks sued through their solicitor, and over a year later, after much bitter argument, agreed to accept £3,450 from the surveyor's insurers. The sum was to cover compensation for the notional difference between the actual cost of the house, and what they would have paid if the defect had been known beforehand – it was not to cover the cost of the repairs. It was also meant to cover legal costs, inconvenience and the return of the fee paid. The Clarks were therefore a good deal out of pocket.

Unfortunately, the law is not particularly kind to the home-owner who finds himself the victim of a negligent surveyor; in most cases he will not receive full compensation for his loss. This is because he is not legally entitled to recover the cost incurred by carrying out the repairs necessary to remedy the defect that the surveyor failed to spot. Instead, he is limited to a sum which reflects the difference between what he actually paid for the property, and what the Court thinks he would have paid had he known of the defect at the time he bought it. Invariably this works out at less than the cost of the repairs, because a vendor would be unlikely to reduce his price to the extent of their full cost – he would argue that he had already taken some account of defects and age when fixing the price of his house in the first place, and if he had been expected to replace all the windows he would have asked a correspondingly higher price.

The injustice to the home-owner is sometimes made worse by the fact that very often he hasn't the money to pay for the repairs and has to borrow from the bank in order to pay the bill. Meanwhile the surveyor, who is doing a ventriloquist act with his insurers, carries on with his surveys, charging higher fees to pay for his increased insurance premiums. The law is therefore most unfair to victims of negligence; in limiting them in this way it totally ignores the reality of the situation.

In 1988 the Royal Institution of Chartered Surveyors set up a 'cut-price' arrangement which enabled house-buyers to take disputes about house surveys to arbitration. At the time of writing solicitors are making hay with a flood of complaints about homes found to contain undisclosed faults after the buyer has moved in. At present the scheme only applies to those buyers to whom reports are addressed – not the valuation reports addressed to building societies and banks. The scheme is aimed at straightforward disputes; it does not cover sharp practice or dishonesty by agents, and it is limited to England and Wales. There is no option to sue once a decision has been made!

Some surveyors, in order to escape their liabilities or at least to reduce them, do their utmost to dissuade the purchaser from buying the property – and if the sale goes ahead in spite of an adverse report, they have avoided liability by having blackened the property. If the sale is abandoned, they still collect their fee, and their responsibility ends at once. There was the instance of one chartered surveyor who was renowned in his area as a 'hard' surveyor. He inspected the roof of a house and advised his client that it was likely to 'slip' at any time. His client promptly called off the deal. The roof, however, was only six years old and a structural analysis subsequently carried out by a structural engineer showed that not only was it impossible for that roof to slip, but furthermore it was twice as strong as the Building Regulations required. The roof was slightly unusual due to the relative heights of the eaves and the ridge, but to a structural engineer the design was sound and anyway was one that had been used many times before. The surveyor was not 'hard' – he was incompetent.

What redress has the unfortunate vendor in such circumstances? None . . .

And can you, if you have a report, sell it if you no longer wish to buy the property? No, you can't! Reports are for the sole benefit of the person to whom they are addressed, and no responsibility is accepted to any third party without prior written consent.

Multiple surveys, which are a feature of the Scottish system, are a problem in England and Wales too. They may be good business for surveyors, but they are a waste of money for those buyers who are unsuccessful or who have to pull out for one reason or another.

CAN I DO MY OWN SURVEY?

You *can* always do your own survey, even though your bank or building society will insist on its own mortgage survey. You will need:

(a) to have good eyesight (or good specs) for seeing close up and in the distance;
(b) to be able to bend and crawl on your hands and knees in the roof space;
(c) to be suspicious and have a good nose for smell;
(d) to ask questions and listen to the answers;
(e) to be thorough and methodical;
(f) to be ready to seek further advice if you run into problems.

Don't be put off by the thought that this is no job for the novice – not everything in surveys is a matter of technical knowledge. Take boundaries, for instance. I once bought a mill house from a family in Cumbria, and during my survey found that a part of the land they were selling did not legally belong to them since it was not on the original conveyance from the lord of the manor. The problem had

You've come to do a survey?

arisen because the first plan used had a river running through the property – what no-one had realised was that the course of the river had changed, leaving a piece of land unconveyed. When this was pointed out, the family's reaction was at first disbelief and then concern, because the sale would have fallen through on this point, especially as, when they acquired the property, they had used a solicitor and a surveyor. In the event, that solicitor was able to obtain the agreement of the lord of the manor to convey the piece of land in question as a separate transaction, and he bore the costs himself. Remember, therefore – it is the land that is conveyed, not the house, so your survey must include the land and its boundaries.

Nearly all structural faults can be detected by the senses, whether they appear as cracks and bulges in the walls, splits and rot in timber, or sagging floors and roofs. It is therefore essential that you are able to note these by

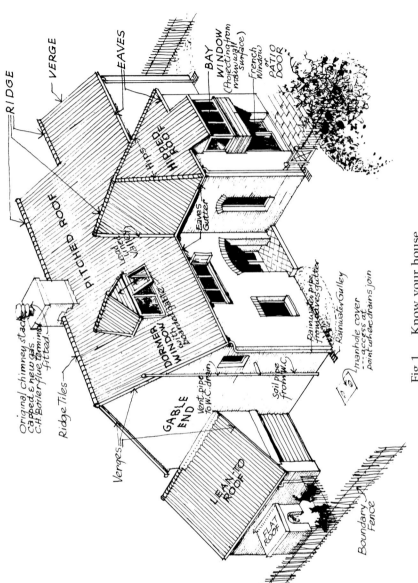

RIDGE

VERGE

EAVES

Original chimney stack.
Capped & new gas
C.H. Boiler flue lining
fitted

Ridge Tiles

PITCHED ROOF

HIPS

HIPPED ROOF

Lead lined
valley

DORMER
WINDOW
with nashing
boards

GABLE
END

Verges

Vent pipe
to W.C. drain

Soil pipe
from W.C.

LEAN-TO
ROOF

FLAT
ROOF

BAY
WINDOW
(Projecting from
main wall
surface)

French
Window

PATIO
DOOR

Eaves
Gutter

Rainwater pipe
from eaves gutter

Rainwater Gulley

manhole cover
— access at
point where drains join

Boundary
Fence

Fig 1   Know your house

systematic observation. What to do after spotting a possible defect? It is a matter for further investigation, but if it looks wrong, it *is* wrong until proved otherwise.

Some defects like damp can be detected by observation, feel and smell. Surveyors use a moisture meter; it is not infallible but is quick and therefore extremely useful if you are able to buy, borrow or hire one. If you have an electrical test meter you can devise one of your own, using two electrodes and measuring the current passing between them when pressed into a wall. A dry wall will not give a reading; a wet one will.

Other defects such as rot can be detected by probing with a screwdriver. The checking of boundaries to see if the land being conveyed is correct requires the ability to understand a simple plan and to measure. You will also need to check the measurements of rooms, which are usually inaccurate in agents' particulars.

Wood and damp treatment guarantees and any service agreements should be examined to see the conditions and exclusions. You may need to seek the advice of wood treatment/damp treatment firms, who will carry out a free survey for you (subject to the agreement of the vendor). The Gas and Electricity Boards will also give you a short visual report on their installations in the house, for a small fee.

You will need to visit the Council offices to check with the building inspector and planning officer whether there is any general problem of drainage or flooding. These officers are remarkably helpful over all such matters, and freely offer their knowledge.

Obviously it helps if you have some building or DIY knowledge, and clearly some defects require further examination by an expert, but a surveyor may not be any better since his knowledge of structures and services is limited.

Even if you have to pay for specialist advice you will still save money if you can do your own survey – moreover you will be in control, and you will gain a knowledge of the house you are buying before your are committed, which could save you a great deal of money and anxiety.

What you want to know is:

Is the building structurally sound and weatherproof?
How much will have to be spent on it?
What exactly is being conveyed, and what are the boundaries and covenants which will affect you?
Is it really suitable for your needs?

Take things logically. Start at the beginning by assessing your situation and requirements. What kind of house do you want? What do you need? (which is not the same thing!) Where should it be? Don't waste time and money on house surveys until these questions have been examined thoroughly.

2 · Choosing, Viewing, Buying

Choosing your house · The cardinal rule · Costs ·
Preliminary inspection · Making an offer · Auctions

A home in which you and your family feel secure and
happy will depend on the wisdom of your choice and an
element of luck. It is impossible to foresee how life will
work out, but a reasonable attempt should at least be made
to avoid the obvious pitfalls. A house is also a major
investment, usually paid for with borrowed money, and
will probably dominate your budget for years to come.

CHOOSING YOUR HOUSE

What is the point of buying a house, even if it is structurally
sound, if it isn't suitable for you or your family? Surveys
carried out by professional surveyors really begin too late
in the house-buying process, and are divorced from the
circumstances of the purchaser and from the legal provisions contained in the deeds and conveyance. This is
wrong. The buyer is in fact the only one in a position to
begin right at the beginning, to make the preliminary
inspections or surveys which should then culminate in the
detailed survey at the end – the final chance to say 'yes',
'no' or 'maybe'.

Moreover, whatever your age, circumstances and

GODS·PROVIDENCE·IS·MINE·INHERITANCE

Plenty of character but expensive to maintain!

financial resources, taking stock is something which must be done from time to time – it is the first step in making decisions. You should review your situation, think about changes, look into the past, present and future, think of the snags, revise your plans – and only then get cracking!

So often people will purchase a five-bedroomed house so that when the sons or daughters get married and have children they can all stay at the family residence at weekends and holiday times. And so often things don't work out quite like this – either the offspring move abroad or, worse still, fall out with their parents who are then left with a house too large for them, but are either unable or unwilling to move to something more suitable.

It would therefore be foolish to make decisions without considering the facts realistically and reducing the un-knowns to a minimum. 'You cannot guarantee success, but you can deserve it' Winston Churchill once wrote.

If you wish to move, where should you go? And what should you buy? How long will it take and what will it cost? Think about any alterations you may wish to make in your lifestyle and the possible snags. This is the initial step in making a plan and ultimately a successful purchase.

You could make a chart showing how you spend your time, and particularly how your leisure time is divided between domestic chores, car maintenance, TV, videos, taking the children out, the pub, visiting friends and relatives, and so on. You might perhaps like it to change: more active pursuits such as walking, golf, tennis, swimming, cycling? Less travelling to work, more visiting, less TV, less time on shopping?

Ask each one of the family to make a list of how they spend their time and what changes they would like to make if given the chance. The results might be surprising and you will certainly feel different about some aspects of life!

Budgeting

Check your spending – perhaps list the things on which your money is spent under three headings. First – the lump sums which turn up regularly such as mortgage, community charge, fuel and water bills, car tax and insurances. Second – the day-to-day expenditure such as food, drink, household goods, newspapers, petrol or bus fares. Third – the occasional sums needed for holidays, car repairs, house repairs, and replacement of furniture and domestic appliances.

So before making the ultimate decision on a new home, just run a check over your budget and see how the new house or flat would affect it. Would your spending pattern have to be rearranged to cope with the increased mortgage? Is your income likely to increase? Is redundancy, early retirement, or any other major change possible or likely in the foreseeable future? Can you afford the repairs to put the proposed property in good order? Your survey will indicate how much you will need to set aside.

Locations and Houses

The next step could be to set down the factors which are important about where you live and then award them points on a sliding scale, ten for the very important, down to one. Here are some to consider:

Access to place of work and schools

People of neighbourhood

Public transport

Access to family, friends, and leisure activities

Opportunities for walking and exercise

Access to shops and health services

The weather (there are marked local differences even in a small area, depending on hills, rivers and buildings)

Now make another table of what you expect from your house, and award points from one to ten in the same way:

Four bedrooms	Well maintained
Modern	Well heated and insulated
Detached, semi, flat or maisonette	Character
Large garden	Large kitchen
Garage	Utility room
Mortgage	Dining room
Outlook	Somewhere to put the Steinway grand!
Privacy	TV and stereo reception

So, having assessed the relative importance of the place and the house in which you would like to live, tables such as these should also help to assess the particular locations and houses which seem attractive, and you can then score the extent to which they fulfil your requirements. Of course, this is only a guide – much of the merit is in doing the exercise itself and thinking about the points raised.

THE CARDINAL RULE

If you make the wrong decision it may seem like the end of the world, but it is not – it can always be put right by moving again! But this brings me to the cardinal rule when buying – always choose a house which will be easy to sell. It should be well located and of sound and durable construction; it should not have too many drawbacks, and these can be wide ranging – the most obvious examples are traffic noise (particularly from motorways or airports), inconsiderate neighbours, shared access, pubs and car parks, and vandalism.

COSTS

Two questions will doubtless be uppermost: how much will it cost, and how can you find the money for it? Remember that the total cost for buying and selling includes:

The agreed purchase price

Solicitor's charges, such as the conveyance fee, fees in connection with your mortgage, fees in connection with selling your present house (about 1%)

Land Registry fee (about ¼%)

Stamp Duty, if over £30,000 (1%)

Building society's valuation survey fee (about £100)

Structural survey fee (if at all)

Repairs, alterations and redecoration

Carpets and curtains etc

Cost of removal

Agent's fees on sale of house (between 1% and 2%)

VAT on fees, repairs, etc

Insurance payment on house (payable at 'Exchange of Contracts' stage)

Leaving aside repairs, alterations, carpets and curtains, these costs could amount to £4,000 on a £75,000 house – a substantial figure. All the more important that you should choose wisely and know what the cost of any anticipated repairs will be.

Looking from the Outside

When you have a list of 'probables', don't waste time viewing inside them all, but leave the car if you have one, and walk the neighbourhood. Look at each probable (and possible) house in its setting from as many viewpoints as

A well maintained chimney with sculptured pots adds interest to a house

A defective boxed-in gutter can cause serious damp problems if not attended to

you can. A map is essential at this stage – after all, there might be a motorway at the bottom of the garden. Study a local map and the Ordnance Survey, which is a mine of information.

Many houses on your list will become rejects purely because of the drawbacks of their location. It may also be possible to get some idea of the neighbours, and whether they keep two caravans or a motorboat in front of the lounge windows. For the full effect of neighbours, go on Saturday or Sunday so as to find the whole array of cars, vans, lorries, motorbikes and children, although if it is a fine weekend some of the boats and caravans may be missing.

It should now be possible to narrow down your choice, but look at your checklist again and again – compare the numbers of rooms and their sizes; consider the garages – gardens – parking space. Is the street safe for children? Are the shops or buses close at hand?

PRELIMINARY INSPECTION

When you view the houses on your shortlist note their age and the materials they are made of. Also, try to make a very rough sketch of the rooms on each floor. It need not be accurate so long as it shows the disposition of the rooms – information which will be of great value later. Room sizes are usually provided on the particulars, and a better sketch can be drawn at home. It is surprising how little will actually be remembered about a house after you have left it, so make as many notes as possible as you go round.

As well as noting down what strikes you as important, try to answer the question, is it right for me and my family? Are the bedrooms large enough to contain, say, two single beds? Is the living room the right shape, facing south and with a pleasant view? If you like a fire, is there a chimney?

Are you going to eat in the living room, dining room or kitchen? Are the kitchen and utility room large enough to take your washing machine, dryer, freezer, refrigerator, etc? Can you install a shower if one is not already there? Is there room for a cubicle or can one be installed over the bath? Is there enough storage space? Remember those difficult objects like prams, bicycles, toys, gardening equipment, golf clubs.

Is the garage large enough for your BMW? Can you get in and out of the car at one side? Is there room for a bench? Is there a power and water point? Try to visualise where your furniture will fit in the house. What about that piano? Ours requires a space 9 × 6ft (2·7 × 1·8m) and needs plenty of light – many are the houses we've rejected because they couldn't take the grand piano!

Never, never make an offer or agree to buy after only one visit. See all the houses on your shortlist first, consider them all carefully, go through the checklist again, and then if one of them seems suitable and you feel in your bones that you would like it, then make a further appointment to view it again.

Second Inspection

This time you must be even more observant. Remember that afterwards you may be making an offer, so a more careful visual inspection must be made at this stage, and the matters only briefly considered on your first visit should be looked at in more depth now. You will need to inspect the roof space, the walls, floors and ceilings, and the staircase; the outside walls, the roof and the chimney; the aerials, drains, garage and outbuildings; the fences and hedges; the gas, electricity, telephone and water mains.

In the roof space, check the thickness of the insulation (the standard is now 100mm/4in); look carefully for signs of woodworm, particularly around the hatch, and for any signs of damp entering through the roof covering, especially at the eaves. So far as the timber structure is concerned, you may not understand it, but it should look regular and well formed. Inspect the water tank to see if it is sound and well insulated.

Walls inside and outside should be inspected for large cracks. On a new house one expects to see shrinkage cracks

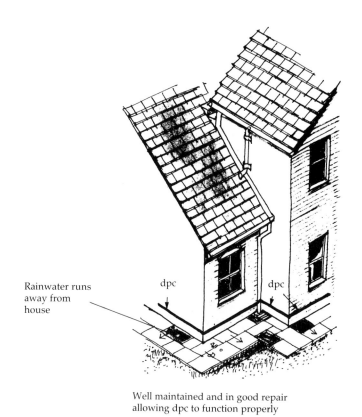

Rainwater runs
away from
house

dpc

dpc

Well maintained and in good repair
allowing dpc to function properly

Fig 2a   Well maintained

in the plaster on walls and ceilings, but not on the outside. Any external crack could have important implications.

Ask the vendors why they are leaving. Have they already a house to go to? What is their programme for moving? – and so on. Press them carefully on the subject of the neighbours, the boundaries and which fences belong to whom. Make no price offer at this stage, but indicate that

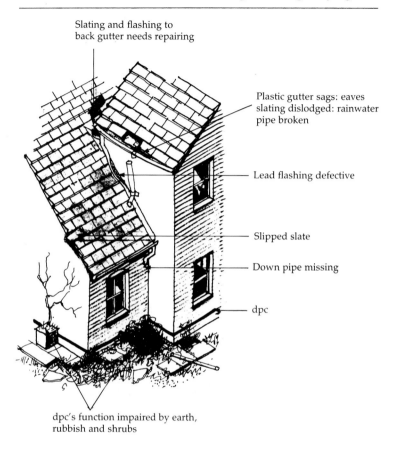

Slating and flashing to
back gutter needs repairing

Plastic gutter sags: eaves
slating dislodged: rainwater
pipe broken

Lead flashing defective

Slipped slate

Down pipe missing

dpc

dpc's function impaired by earth,
rubbish and shrubs

Fig 2b Badly maintained

you might make one after consideration, and having done
some sums. Be friendly and try to give the impression that
you are a person of integrity who knows his or her own
mind, and are not likely to abandon a deal half-way
through. This is particularly important if there are others
bidding for the same house.

Be suspicious of newly painted black beams – they might not be as sound as they seem – especially at the joints

Badly filled joints allow water to enter cavity

MAKING AN OFFER

At home, try to estimate the cost of alterations and repairs, whether this will be in hundreds or thousands, and form a judgement of the value of the house. If you reach the conclusion that the asking price is reasonable, ring the agent and ask if any other offers have been made and what he thinks the owner might accept. It is surprising how frank agents can be sometimes – after all, whatever their clients want, the agents want a quick sale. If there are others interested you could lose the house by trying to reduce the price. On the other hand, if there are no others in the field, an offer of, say, 2½ per cent less than the asking price could be made; and if the house is somewhat overpriced, try an offer between 5 and 10 per cent less than the asking price and see what the reaction is.

If your offer is accepted, the vendor's agent will notify you in writing, and he will also notify the vendor and his solicitor as well as your own solicitor. The legal process of buying then begins.

AUCTIONS

Auctions are quite a different matter. If a house is bought this way *all* the surveys and investigations should be carried out *first*, and you must be ready to sign and exchange contracts on the day of the auction after paying over the 10 per cent deposit. Unless your own house has been sold, or there is sufficient spare cash to buy a second, do not purchase by this method. If you do, bidding can be very exhilarating, and on no account should you bid more than your pre-determined limit. Because it is very tempting to do so, it is often best to ask an estate agent or your solicitor to bid for you.

House-buying is rather like drinking wine. It can be heady stuff, it can be a pleasant experience, or it can leave a nasty taste in the mouth and cost a great deal. The remedy is to keep a clear head and remain in control.

3 · Survey and Sell

Survey technique · Preparation · Choosing an estate agent · Showing round · Sold?

It may seem strange to include this chapter, but there are two reasons. Firstly, here is a chance to practise your survey technique, on the house you are selling. Secondly, it will help you sell it!

SURVEY AND PREPARATION

Long before you put the house on the market, make a thorough survey of the property. Check and repair the roof, woodwork, windows, doors, pointing, plumbing, heating, and so on. Then redecorate where necessary, paying particular attention to the kitchen, bathroom and external window sills.

One other task to carry out well in advance – the garden and exterior maintenance: all fences, gates, paths and steps should be repaired. At the same time, inspect and clean the gutters and rainwater gullies, emptying them of leaves and silt – finish off by flushing them with a bucket of warm water. It is well worth while to lift the manhole covers, then wash the brickwork and the 'benching' with warm water, and point any defective brickwork or joints; replace the covers after smearing the rims with a little grease to prevent them sticking. You may be surprised how impressed some buyers and their surveyors will be with a good clean manhole!

Sturdy suburban house of the 1930's – the best building period before the '80's

The garden itself must look neat and manageable. Grass edges should be trimmed, flowerbeds and vegetable beds cleared of leaves and debris. Colour and foliage can set off the most ordinary-looking house, whereas a poorly kept garden with no trees or shrubs seems to place a dead hand on the house itself. Do not hesitate to ask your friends what they would do – they see your home much as the prospective purchaser will see it.

The front door and porch are particularly important. This is the part of the house that visitors stand closest to and from which they will form their first impression. The 'door furniture' must therefore be attractive and well painted or polished; if it is worn out, then renew it. A shrub on either side or hanging baskets make a strong impact, but beware of coach lanterns and spoked cartwheels. They only appeal to a few, and some people are repelled by them.

A colleague of mine in Buckinghamshire had great difficulty in selling his little terraced house; after months on the market not one person had come further than the front door and he was about to lower the already modest asking price. On being asked about the condition of the front door and windows, he admitted they hadn't been painted for many years and that the door had more or less reached the end of its life, and showed it. I suggested he should replace the door with a new one, re-paint the windows and leave the price as it was. He did this, and within one month had four people to view, one of whom bought the house. So many people will not even bother to look around a place which from the outside looks unattractive and neglected.

The next task is to give the house a thorough spring-clean, paying particular attention to curtains, carpets and polished floors. A feeling of care and freshness should pervade the house. Check the lighting. Table lamps and lamp standards can be used to good effect when showing off the house in the evening or on dark winter afternoons. Each room should be lit with a warm glow, rather than a glaring white light from a central light bulb covered with a scorched paper shade!

CHOOSING AN ESTATE AGENT

Almost a quarter of the people questioned by the Consumers' Association were positively dissatisfied with the service provided by estate agents. Nearly half of those questioned – all of whom had bought or sold property within the past eighteen months – had some complaint, the most common being that agents charged too much and were inefficient or indifferent. The survey, published in 'Which?', showed that the great majority of people still used estate agents although there was widespread dissatisfaction with the system. Eighty-six per cent had used an agent when either buying or selling, and of the sellers, two-thirds had used only one agent.

According to the survey, agents frequently overestimate the size of rooms. The same room in one house had been

described by one agent as 26ft 6in long and 14ft wide (8 ×
4·2m), and by another agent as 19ft 3in long and 15ft 4in
(5·8 × 4·6m) wide.

The crucial choice of an estate agent raises the question
of whether one is necessary at all. Going it alone in difficult
times is not to be recommended, but if you wish to try it
for a few weeks then there is no harm done, simply time
lost if you are unsuccessful. The qualities to look for in an
agent are integrity, power of persuasion and an active
ambition to succeed. In addition, an agent should always
keep his client's interests at the front of his mind.

Make a list of the agents in your area. Select two or three
with a good reputation and go to see them. Make an
appointment to see either a partner or, if it is a large firm,
the local manager. Keep the meeting formal but friendly.
Ask plenty of questions. Ask particulary about fees (1-1½
per cent plus advertising is quite enough to pay).

Invite the chosen agent to inspect the house and give an
indication of the market price. It is of tremendous value to
prepare your own draft of the house description, even
though it is the agent's job to do this. Describe the house
as you would like to see it portrayed. Measure the rooms
carefully; measure the size of the whole plot also.
Remember that someone like yourself is going to buy it, so
put down what you think is important. List the fittings
which are being included in the sale; these are usually items
fixed to the walls such as kitchen units, mirrors, light
fittings, cupboard units and, of course, any curtains or
carpets and so on.

The agent will form an opinion of the top and bottom
prices the house is likely to get and, if he is honest, tell you
the middle price. There is no harm in adding, say, 5% to
that price as long as you are prepared to reduce it by that
amount in negotiation.

SHOWING ROUND

When the great moment arrives and the first prospective
buyer appears, be as cool, calm and collected as possible.

Try to send the children out. If it is dark, switch on subdued lighting in each room, and your red-glow fire in the sitting room if you don't have a 'real' fire. Blow away any cooking smells – other than coffee or newly baked bread in the kitchen! Decide beforehand in which order you will show off the rooms, but always start and finish in the sitting room. Say very little. Mention the local schools, shops and buses if they exist. Do not point out any snags, but answer honestly any questions put to you, and be ready for the 'Why are you moving?' one. If you are not sure of the answers, say so, and leave it at that.

SOLD?

Leave the haggling over the price to your agent and take his advice on the final choice of buyer, who should be well advanced in his own sale; but do not be in any hurry to settle the matter without at least sleeping on it and allowing for second thoughts all round. When the price has been agreed your agent will confirm it in writing and notify your solicitor – but wait until the buyer's survey has been completed and the house given the OK before celebrating or allowing your agent to put up his 'Sold Subject to Contract' sign.

4 · Building and Structural Defects

BRE Investigation · Woodworm and Fungal Decay of Timber · Dampness and Condensation · Roofs Foundations and Walls

---

BRE INVESTIGATION

An investigation by the Building Research Establishment a few years ago identified over a thousand different kinds of faults in new homes under construction. Their report, 'Quality in Traditional Housing', indicated that half the faults concerned the external walls, roofs, windows and doors and related to durability and performance. They also found that Building Regulations and Codes of Practice were regularly infringed, and experience suggests that a considerable number of faults had been concealed.

This comes as no surprise to the house-owner, and is only the culmination of years of dissatisfaction with the building industry. We are constantly reminded of the appalling condition of our houses. Leaking roofs, rotting window frames, condensation, cracked walls and ceilings, and inadequate heating systems are a feature of daily living. The Building Research Establishment suggested that more emphasis should be placed on frequent inspection by architects and builders.

A synopsis in table form of the faults listed in the report is set out overleaf.

Line and level are all-important for sound walls

Stone sills and treated timber are a sound combination, but workmanship is important too

Synopsis in Table Form

The faults listed and categorised in the report included the following:

BELOW THE DAMP-PROOF COURSE

Inadequate mortar filling of cavities

Poor quality of bricks, blocks and mortar

Drains underneath foundations subject to damage

Quality of hardcore defective

Damp-proof membranes not continuous and sometimes missing

Mature trees too close

Water penetration through door thresholds

UP TO ROOF LEVEL

Wall cavities bridged

Poor quality and damaged bricks used in external walls

Joints between windows and walls too large or unfilled

Inadequate quality of materials used in floors and ceilings – thickness, knots, durability

Floor joists bowing – high moisture content

Corrodable fixings in external walls

Inadequate window sills

Roof straps and hangers bent, mispositioned or inadequate

Timber untreated

Gaps in walls

FINISHINGS

Faults with boilers

Electric sockets and fittings inconvenient, dangerous or mispositioned

Inadequate width of staircases and landings

Staircase handrails rough or flimsy

Poor quality of doors and windows

Non-safety glass in high-risk areas

Painted finishes to windows and doors defective

EXTERNAL

Paving faults – incorrect falls, bedding

Walls to porches not weatherproofed

Inadequate support to porch roofs

Rainwater pipes and gutters missing or inadequately jointed

This chapter concentrates on those important aspects of building and building damage with which you should be familiar before you can begin surveying.

WOODWORM AND FUNGAL DECAY OF TIMBER

This subject may send shivers down your spine, but you are right to be alarmed, for whether it is the lowly woodworm or the dreaded deathwatch beetle, whether it is dry rot or wet rot, all weaken the structural timbers of a dwelling. The good news is that the most common infestation, by the woodworm – or *anobium punctatum* or furniture beetle, call it what you will – can be treated, so long as it has not gone too far into the timbers, at a cost of a few hundred pounds. Treatment involves the application

Too risky to leave to chance – lift the small section of floorboards and examine the joists

Roof ventilation blocked by insulation at eaves – fungal decay developing

of insecticide by pressure spray in the form of pungent solvents or water-based emulsions or pastes. Timber can usually be treated in situ, so if you detect or suspect infestation it is best to obtain a survey from a reputable timber treatment firm (or more than one), who will provide a 30-year guarantee of their treatment. Even if there is no suspected infestation, these firms will usually carry out a no-cost survey, often recommending a precautionary treatment (and guarantee).

Dry rot is disastrous, and any house you encounter with it should be left strictly to the experts, the treatment involving extensive renewal of timbers and the disinfecting of all other timbers, brickwork, slates and cavities.

Timbers affected by wet rot need only to be dried out, or cut out and replaced with sound timbers, and so long as the source of wetting is removed and air allowed to circulate, the rot will not recur.

The most serious attack by wood-boring beetles can cause structural damage, but this is rare except in older houses, nearly all of which have some kind of local attack. This applies equally to newer houses, the infestation often being brought in with furniture. The conditions which encourage attack are moisture and lack of good ventilation, but the common furniture beetle, the House Longhorn, thrives in dry internal conditions and is often found in skirtings, door frames, pelmets, under stairs and around trap-doors. The tell-tale signs are pin holes and dust in both soft- and hardwoods; the mighty deathwatch beetle leaves larger holes in hardwoods such as elm and oak.

Be systematic with your inspection: test all easily accessible timbers with a sharp screwdriver to detect concealed tunnels and boreholes; lift some carpets and where possible a section of floorboards, and test the joists. If there is any infestation at all, you can be certain that there is more undetected, and that treatment by a specialist firm will be essential. Ventilation is very important, therefore in any place where this is absent – such as around floor joists and in roof spaces – suspect the worst.

Wet rot is obvious if the timbers are wet, but they may

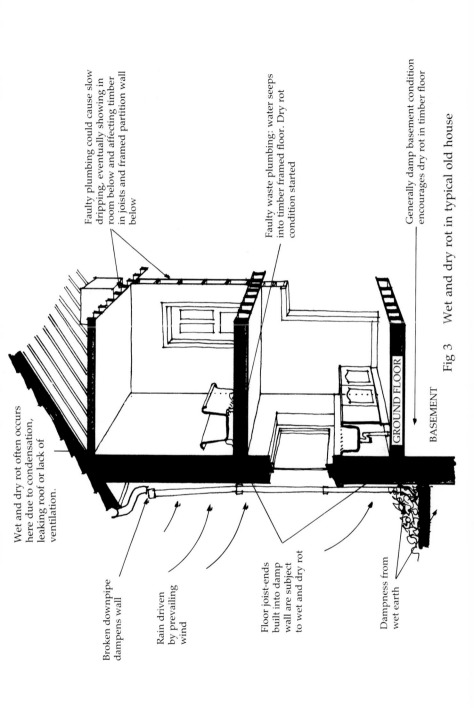

Wet and dry rot often occurs here due to condensation, leaking roof or lack of ventilation.

Faulty plumbing could cause slow dripping, eventually showing in room below and affecting timber in joists and framed partition wall below

Faulty waste plumbing; water seeps into timber framed floor. Dry rot condition started

Generally damp basement condition encourages dry rot in timber floor

GROUND FLOOR

BASEMENT

Broken downpipe dampens wall

Rain driven by prevailing wind

Floor joist-ends built into damp wall are subject to wet and dry rot

Dampness from wet earth

Fig 3   Wet and dry rot in typical old house

have dried out so watch for stain marks and test the ends of joists, beams and trusses with a screwdriver to see if they are soft or brittle.

Dry rot smells fusty and has white cobweb-pattern marks. If tested with a screwdriver the wood will break away (– remember to disinfect the screwdriver and your hands afterwards). Pay particular attention to the ends of joists in contact with brickwork, check under staircases, in cellars and in all built-in cupboards or 'dead' spaces. Poor ventilation and damp will almost certainly be the prime causes.

And one word of warning! Don't accept a wood treatment guarantee as proof that infestation has been eliminated; re-infestation has been found rife in a roof space only five years after it had been treated. The guarantee only agrees to *re-treat* the affected areas – it does not guarantee that the problem will not recur. Any sign of infestation calls for inspection and treatment by a reputable and approved wood treatment company, one that is likely to stay in existence for as long as its guarantee period.

For further reading there is an excellent publication available from the Building Research Establishment's Princes Risborough Laboratory, Aylesbury, Bucks HP17 9PX, called *'Recognising Wood Rot and Insect Damage in Building'*.

DAMPNESS AND CONDENSATION

When it comes to dampness, all is not always what it seems, so don't automatically assume that a damp patch is due to a defective damp-proof course (dpc). It could be due to defective plumbing, such as a leaking water pipe, gutters, downpipes, lead flashings, blocked wall cavities, driving rain (where there are solid walls) or even just condensation on cold surfaces.

Most buildings before the turn of the century were built without dpc's, which are simply layers of impervious material such as slate, copper, bituminous felt, heavy gauge plastic or, in special circumstances, 'engineering' bricks

Gullies must be securely bedded, joined and sealed to avoid rainwater seeping into foundations

such as Staffordshire blues.

Unfortunately even where fitted, dpc's can easily be fractured or by-passed by ground movement, bad workmanship or by the plain ignorance of builders or owners.

The dpc is inserted in all walls, internal and external, 6 to 12in (15 to 30cm) above ground level. It must be continuous around the walls, so on a sloping site it will step up and down along the joints in the brickwork. It is essential to locate the dpc to ensure it really is at least 6in (15cm) above ground level and has not been submerged below paving, flower beds, piles of rubbish or suchlike. Nor should external rendering override the damp-proof membrane. If the house has a solid floor, that too must have a

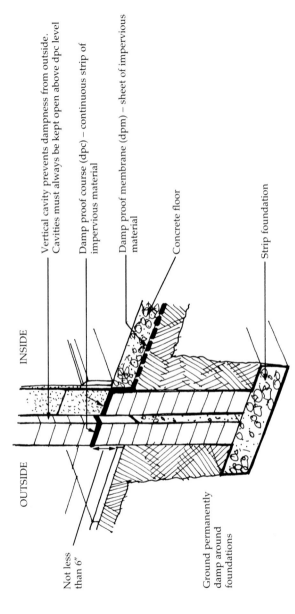

OUTSIDE

INSIDE

Vertical cavity prevents dampness from outside. Cavities must always be kept open above dpc level

Damp proof course (dpc) – continuous strip of impervious material

Damp proof membrane (dpm) – sheet of impervious material

Concrete floor

Strip foundation

Not less than 6"

Ground permanently damp around foundations

NB Cavity and dpc together exclude dampness from interior of house

Fig 4   Cavity wall and dpc

membrane which extends over the whole of it, and although it is not possible to see it, any defects will show in the form of damp patches under floor coverings, discolouration or loose vinyl tiles.

Once damp has affected walls it deposits hygroscopic salts on the surface, leaving white salty tidemarks which make detection all the easier. Rising damp is *only* found at ground level, petering out and fading some three or four feet (about a metre) up the walls. Internally it tends to cause wallpaper to lift off, to soften plaster and flake emulsion paint, leaving tidemarks. Tapping the wall with the handle of a screwdriver often produces a dull, hollow sound which can help to determine the extent of the area affected.

Damp patches elsewhere, especially if they occur after rain, are usually due to defective roof drainage and flashings around chimneys. A damp patch on a chimney breast can also be due to condensation forming within the flue, especially if it is a disused chimney with fireplaces blocked up. Such a chimney should always be ventilated by an air grill at its base and the pot should be protected from rain entering, though any cover must still allow the chimney to breathe.

Condensation can form anywhere, but is particularly prevalent in moist conditions where ventilation is poor and where heat is absent or kept to a minimum. It occurs in kitchens, bathrooms, rooms not in general use, behind wardrobes and around windows. It is often difficult to distinguish from damp caused by the entry of rain and ground water, but it is nearly always accompanied by the formulation of mould – usually green/black. Salt analysis will provide conclusive proof. Rising damp may be rare in newer buildings but condensation is common. Cellars have both!

To cure condensation, the mould has to be killed off with a bleach solution, and then warmth and ventilation increased. Some cold walls, especially in old houses with solid walls, draw atmospheric moisture to them, rather as windows do. Air bricks, extractor fans, open fires and dehumidifiers all help, but often you have to learn to live

A stepped foundation and dpc on a sloping site

Creeper can damage your brickwork and cause damp

Damp due to conden-
sation or defective
window seal

with it – and there is nothing worse than a new house
which was built in wet conditions. I have known the
condensation problems associated with 'drying out' to last
at least two summers.

There are a number of treatments for rising damp, but the
most common (and cheapest) treatment is by silicone
injection, carried out by a specialist firm and carrying a 30-
year guarantee. A continuous series of 15mm (½in)
diameter holes is drilled into the wall near dpc level and a
silicone resin fed in to soak into the brick or stonework. This
then forms a solidified jelly impervious to water. After the
new dpc has been installed it is essential to remove all the
old plaster from the affected areas and replace it with a
special waterproof plaster developed for the purpose.

Tell-tale holes above the dpc indicate that silicone-injection treatment has been applied to the wall

As above, but the cause of dampness is probably the paving being raised almost to dpc level – it should be at least six inches below it

To sum up, damp walls are not disastrous structurally, but the cause must be ascertained and the condition rectified. Correct analysis is important. The cause may be difficult to diagnose and costly to correct, and internal decorations are easily spoilt. Therefore detection of damp in a survey calls for further examination and report (usually free) by a specialist contractor, who should be a member of the British Chemical Damp Proof Association.

ROOFS

Structure

The roof structure provides the base to which insulating and roof covering materials can be attached in order to keep the building weathertight. It keeps the whole roof in position and transmits its weight, and the considerable windloadings it is subjected to, through the walls and down to the foundations. The windloadings vary from extreme downward pressures to reversals causing upward suction. The structure must therefore be secured firmly to the walls through timber 'wall-plates' which run horizontally around the top of the brickwork, and all the elements – battens, rafters, trusses, purlins and wallplates – must be securely fastened to each other as well as to the walls.

The design and size of the roof timbers is governed by the Building Regulations and approved by the local authority. Most roofs exceed these minimum requirements, but if they are inadequate or have been seriously affected by bad workmanship, poor quality timber, woodworm, dry rot, wet rot, and so on, the eventual result is seen in sagging roofs, displaced or split timbers, twisted and open joints – and visible movement of walls at eaves level. Watch out for all of them!

Coverings

Roof coverings on pitched roofs are usually of concrete or clay tiles or slates, all of which deteriorate with age and

Fig 5   Common roof types
(a) Hipped roof

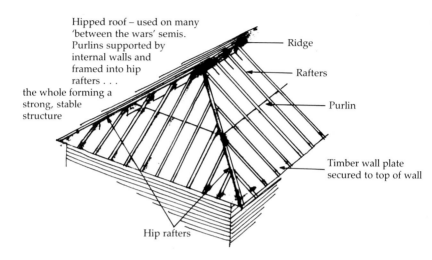

Hipped roof – used on many
'between the wars' semis.
Purlins supported by
internal walls and
framed into hip
rafters . . .
the whole forming a
strong, stable
structure

Ridge

Rafters

Purlin

Timber wall plate
secured to top of wall

Hip rafters

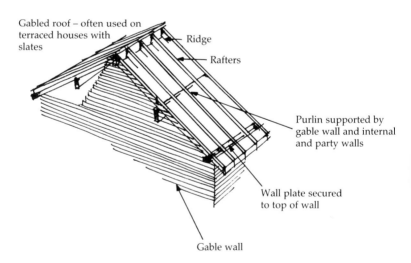

Gabled roof – often used on
terraced houses with
slates

Ridge

Rafters

Purlin supported by
gable wall and internal
and party walls

Wall plate secured
to top of wall

Gable wall

(b) Gabled roof

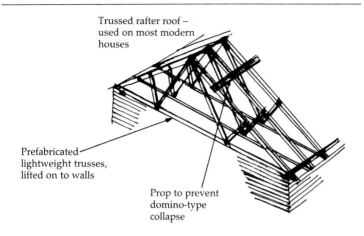

Trussed rafter roof –
used on most modern
houses

Prefabricated
lightweight trusses,
lifted on to walls

Prop to prevent
domino-type
collapse

(c) Trussed rafter roof

ultimately begin to crumble or split. During the lifetime of
the roof they will have to deal with up to a million gallons
of water and will be subjected to the sun's ultra-violet rays,
frost, snow and wind. Failure to prevent rain entering can
result in damage to the structure beneath, and to ceilings
and decorations.

Missing, slipped or broken slates are a potential source of
trouble, even though the overlap of one slate on another is
more than 50 per cent. Ridge, hip and gable tiles are
commonly displaced by gales, causing accumulation of
debris in gutters, valleys and junctions. Mortar fillets and
flashings around chimneys, bay windows and roof lights
are another common source of trouble. Slipping tiles or
slates may indicate a more serious condition, of 'nail
sickness', where the nails securing the tiles to the wooden
battens have become rusted through or fatigued. If this is
the case the whole roof covering and battens will need to
be replaced.

The installation of slates and tiles in the last 30 or 40 years
has included the fixing of bituminous felt beneath the
battens to afford a further barrier against driven rain, snow,
dust and offensive smells. This also provides some resistance

Foam blocks have been inserted underneath roof slates to prevent slippage – this usually indicates 'nail sickness'

Sound hip rafter and purlins – absence of felt admits dust but allows good ventilation

Roof ventilation blocked by insulation at eaves – fungal decay developing. Note also the loose electric cable

to heat loss. Care should be taken that the lower edge of the draped felt extends beyond the eaves and fascia board into the gutter. The felt layers should be lapped by at least 150mm (6in), the upper felt being placed over the lower felt so that there is a continuous fall towards the eaves gutter. Any rain penetrating the roof covering is then expelled without entering the roof structure.

The nails used to fasten tiles and slates should be of copper or aluminium composition. In some roofs tiles are hung on to the battens with only every third row nailed. If your roof is not felted, it may be a little dustier in the roof space, but it will be better ventilated and you can see what is happening to the tiles and battens more easily. This is not a structural defect – only a sign of antiquity.

Drainage

The roof drainage should be able to take water away quickly and cleanly without obstruction, and therefore eaves tiles should discharge neatly into gutters without water being blown back on to the wall or woodwork. Gutters should be clean and sloping to downpipes and should not have dips. Downpipes should be clean and placed at frequent intervals so as to avoid long gutter runs and changes of direction.

SECTION THROUGH EAVES
LOOKING UP FROM GROUND

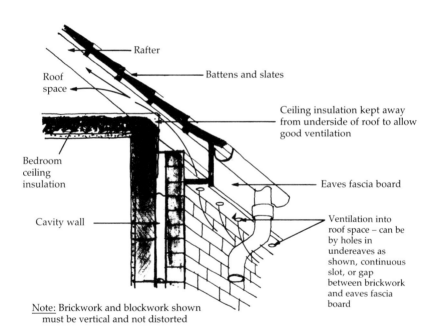

Rafter

Roof space

Battens and slates

Ceiling insulation kept away from underside of roof to allow good ventilation

Bedroom ceiling insulation

Eaves fascia board

Cavity wall

Ventilation into roof space – can be by holes in undereaves as shown, continuous slot, or gap between brickwork and eaves fascia board

Note: Brickwork and blockwork shown must be vertical and not distorted

Fig 6   Insulation and roof ventilation

Roof Insulation

The roof space should be insulated with a glass-fibre quilt at least 100mm (4in) thick and preferably 150mm (6in) thick. This is normally placed between the ceiling joists, but it is essential that the space under the water tank(s) is left un-insulated to allow heat to permeate through the ceiling, and that any water pipes and tanks in the roof space are themselves well insulated. Failure to observe these precautions will almost certainly lead to a freeze-up.

Humid air permeating from below can cause condensation in the roof space, particularly where there is felt under the roof tiles, which can cause the timbers to rot. This can be avoided, however, by ensuring plenty of cross ventilation in the roof all round the eaves and at the gable ends by means of visible gaps, air bricks or ventilators. These ventilation routes must be maintained and kept free of insulation material, birds' nests, junk and so on.

Electric wiring should, if possible, be kept clear of the insulation; and if you are considering having the joists treated for woodworm, all insulation will have to be removed first.

Flat Roofs

The problems associated with felted flat roofs are common knowledge. They can leak when new, they can leak after a few years, and they have a guaranteed life of only 15 years. The reasons for these defects are: inadequate materials which are affected by sunlight and abrasion; poor design such as inadequate flashings and complicated openings for chimneys and gutters; and finally, poor workmanship where the operatives and supervisors have received no formal training. Furthermore, you are entitled to assume that any flat roof will need replacing before long, even if it is only on a garage, porch or dormer window. There are new flat roof systems about which are supposed to be better, but they suffer from the same inherent disadvantages as their earlier counterparts. The materials may well have improved, but only time will tell if the same can

SECTION THROUGH WALL OVER BAY WINDOW

External cavity wall supported by timber beams over bay

Water entry due to faulty flashing or roofing can affect structure

Bay ceiling

Look for signs of dampness on bay ceiling

If entrance porch roof faulty, consider re-roofing in double pitch form (as dotted line)

Use upper windows to inspect lower roofs

For dormer roofs, examine condition of ceiling

Typical felt roofing deterioration – bubbling and cracking and faulty flashing to gable wall: timbers in roof structure may be affected: replace with sloping roof (as dotted line)

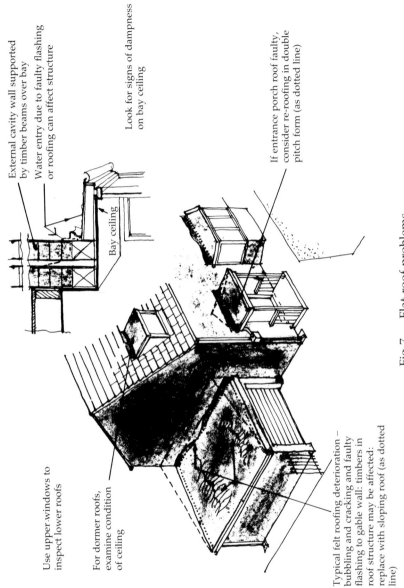

Fig 7   Flat roof problems

be said of workmanship and design.

Not all problems are caused by leaks. Condensation is a common problem. Most roofs are built with an insulating quilt of glass fibre laid on the ceiling boards some distance below the felt surface. It is here that condensation forms unless the space is ventilated – which it hardly ever is. The concealed roof timbers are then subjected to conditions of continual vaporisation and condensation which give rise to wet and dry rot. Most garages escape this problem since usually they have no ceiling boards or insulation and the roof timbers are left exposed.

Blistering of the felt, splits and cracks will occur in most felt roofs and are due to thermal movement and brittleness resulting from exposure to ultra-violet light and locked-in vapours.

Replacement of roofing felt usually also means the replacement of some, at least, of the roof boarding, possibly joists too, and nearly always the insulation.

FOUNDATIONS AND WALLS

Ninety per cent of the cost of major defects under the NHBC warranty scheme, and 20 per cent of all building maintenance arises from faults in foundation design and construction. The major insurance companies receive about 10,000 claims each year, and following the severe drought in 1976 the number doubled. Also following 1976, the Building Regulations required foundations to be deeper to avoid the effects of shrinkage, particularly in clay soils. They should not be less than one metre deep and all peat, silt and made-up ground should be avoided.

Types of Foundations

Foundations can be defined as those parts of the structure in direct contact with the ground which transfer the weight of the building and the loads exerted on it to the soil beneath. Usually we use the term to describe the part of the building or structure from the ground-floor level down-

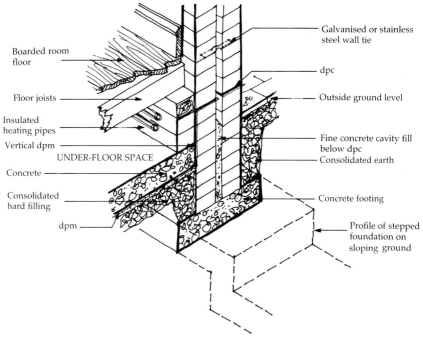

Boarded room floor

Floor joists

Insulated heating pipes

Vertical dpm

UNDER-FLOOR SPACE

Concrete

Consolidated hard filling

dpm

Galvanised or stainless steel wall tie

dpc

Outside ground level

Fine concrete cavity fill below dpc

Consolidated earth

Concrete footing

Profile of stepped foundation on sloping ground

Fig 8   Foundations

wards, and the term 'superstructure' defines the building above this level.

The design of foundations (and superstructure) is specified by the Building Regulations and Codes of Practice. Usually two main types are used – strip foundations and raft foundations. The first, as its name implies, consists of a concrete strip under the load-bearing walls, whereas the raft foundation consists of a reinforced concrete slab under the entire structure. The latter type is used where the ground-bearing properties, ie the safe load which the ground can carry, are low or uneven.

Settlement

All foundations suffer some degree of settlement, since the sub-soil itself is elastic or compressible. Where this is slight or uniformly even no problems arise. Where it is excessive, or where it varies from point to point, problems occur, resulting in cracking, disfigurement and detachment of the walls. Even the drying out of ground beneath boilers can cause shrinkage – which is why boilers should be well insulated at ground level.

Settlement can be downward, or upward (when it is known as 'heave'). In sandy soils settlement is usually even; in clay soils consolidation is slow, uneven and affected by water and dryness causing the clay to expand or contract. Heave can be caused by the ingress of water into clay and by chemical action in certain types of soil and shale filling. The following also affect ground movement: trees and vegetation, changes in water level, landslides, vibrations, mining operations (even some distance away) and flooding.

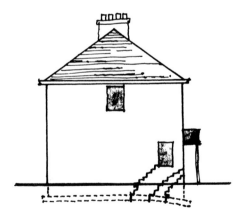

Diagonal cracks where foundation
has given way at one corner only

Fig 9   Foundation defect on corner of house

Swelling cracks due to ground swell under building caused by expansion of clay, tree roots, frost, sulphate attack on concrete, or wrong type of filling under slab

Fig 10   Cracks due to ground swell

Random cracks due to uneven settlement of foundations, caused by shrinkage of clay soils, changes in ground water, consolidation or yielding of subsoil

Fig 11   Random cracks in brickwork

It follows, therefore, that drainage of the ground around the foundations is very important.

Cracking Patterns in Walls

There are a number of typical cracking patterns with various causes which develop in walls and which help the diagnosis of foundation failure, and these are shown in the accompanying illustrations. The Building Research Establishment, in attempting to assess the consequences of cracking, published an assessment of visible damage to walls and plaster. Fine cracks internally visible but not seen externally can be ignored if they are less than 1mm in width and can be filled during redecoration. The occasional hairline crack in external brickwork need not be of any significance, but should be observed over a period to see if it extends or widens. However, *numerous* external small cracks or a single large crack are signs of movement which need expert investigation by a structural engineer.

Where failure is due to inadequate foundations, and where neither the cause nor the effect can be eliminated, then underpinning will stabilise the building and restore its use and value. Underpinning is expensive and inconvenient, and involves the addition of new foundations or short concrete piles without demolishing the building.

Clay Soils

Clay soils undergo a considerable change in volume. Some clays are worse than others, and among those with a high risk are: Ampthill, Gault, Kimmeridge, London, Oxford, Reading, Wadhurst and Weald clays, with up to 100mm (4in) differential settlements being observed.

Trees such as poplars, elms, limes and oaks account for much shrinkage in soil and should not be closer to the building than 1·5 times their own height. If trees are young they should be removed, but with mature trees felling can lead to ground recovery and swell as moisture returns, thus causing even worse damage. A better solution is to prune roots and branches.

Underpinning and extending, using short bored piles

Cavity Walls and Wall Ties

Before 1930 most houses were built with solid brick walls.
Since then, cavity walls have been the norm as they offer
better resistance to rain and damp penetration and have
better sound and thermal characteristics. Above dpc level
both the outer leaf of facing bricks, and the inner and
thicker leaf of common bricks or blocks, are built as
independent structures separated by a cavity 2 to 4in (50 to
100mm) wide. The two leaves are, however, linked across
the cavity with metal wall ties so as to stabilise them, and
particularly the narrower outer leaf; the ties are firmly
bedded in the mortar of both leaves. Over the years these
have come in a variety of shapes, sizes and materials: mild
steel, galvanised steel, cast iron, copper, aluminium and
stainless steel. The most common in use are strips or wires
of galvanised steel. Their quality and spacing is laid down

in the Building Regulations, but in the last ten years difficulties have arisen over corrosion, not only in those made of mild steel but also in galvanised ties where the zinc coating is defective. Corrosion is severest closer to the outer leaf where damp is more severe and where the rust expands, forcing open the mortar joints, and in extreme cases causing bulging and cracking of the wall which is visible externally.

Horizontal cracking is usually evident at about every sixth course of bricks. The stability of the wall is obviously affected, and if left untreated may lead to eventual collapse. If corrosion is suspected, a structural engineer or specialist contractor should be asked to report. He will drill small holes and insert an endoscope, a thin optical instrument with a light at one end which enables him to inspect the cavity. Treatment will involve either removing patches of brickwork and inserting new ties, or inserting stainless steel bolts especially developed for the purpose. The specialist contractor offers a complete service of diagnosis and repair, with guarantees.

The quality of materials used in walls is governed by the Building Regulations, but the walls themselves may be built of bricks, blocks, stone, concrete or timber. In all new buildings they should carry guarantees of quality and certificates of compliance with Building Regulations, Codes of Practice and British Standards. In older buildings they should show no sign of crumbling, disintegration, staining or distortion, no matter what their age. Surveys of houses showing this kind of distress should be left strictly to the structural engineer, as should prefabricated concrete houses, and those made of wattle and clay (there are some!).

Cavity Insulation

As already stated, the primary function of cavity walls is to prevent rain or moisture absorbed by the outer leaf from affecting the inner leaf with its internal plaster and decorations. Above the dpc a continuous space of 2 to 4in

Defective pointing reduces strength of wall

(50 to 100mm) is provided between the two leaves. As well as these weather-resisting advantages, the cavity wall has greater sound and thermal insulating properties and a greater resistance to overturning. It also has other economic advantages in that it requires fewer facing bricks than solid walls!

Now, if you fill the cavity there is a danger that you negate the primary object of keeping out damp, and this is the main reason why architects and surveyors are none too

Beyond your competence – leave this foundation
failure to a structural engineer

happy with the technique. Tests on earlier buildings so
treated revealed that up to one in twenty houses soon
showed signs of damp penetration. Urea formaldehyde foam
used to be the most common and the cheapest method, but
this is not recommended now for use in high exposure areas
such as hillsides, or in tall buildings. There is also a slight
risk of the foam emitting fumes into the living areas, especially in timber-frame houses. Other materials such as blown

mineral wool and blown polystyrene beads do not have this disadvantage if expertly installed, but the beads can be a nuisance if ever the wall needs to be pierced.

Incidentally, cavity wall insulation should be impermeable to water *vapour*, or interstitial condensation can occur. Therefore, check cavity-filled walls carefully for damp patches *anywhere*, and ensure that they have been sealed effectively at the eaves to prevent any fumes escaping into the roof space. Personally I would leave the filling of cavities to the dentist!

5 · Flats, Party Walls and Timber-Frame Houses

Flats and Party Walls · Timber-Frame controversy · Using Timber-Frame · Official Reports

FLATS AND PARTY WALLS

Problems arise from the fact that the repair responsibilities of landlord and lessee are shared. There is no common form of lease, but usually, quite apart from the flat itself, the lessee is responsible for a proportion of the cost of repair of the common parts, which include such costly items as roofs, staircases, lifts, boilers, foundations, gardens and external decoration. You must establish the extent of these liabilities with your solicitor, but even then you can only carry out an inspection limited to your particular flat, plus a superficial investigation of the common parts with the landlord's permission.

No-one whose home floats several floors above the ground can be said to own that home, since the law of England and Wales ties ownership rights to the *land*! The freeholder of the land has the right of entry whether the occupant of the flat is renting by the week or has a 99-year lease. Flat-ownership in Scotland means just that – ownership in perpetuity. Reform is overdue and will come –

Flats? Who pays for remedial work to the concrete structure? Note the rusting reinforcement with inadequate protection

sometime. However, flats or terraced houses, or even semis, are interdependent buildings sharing common walls and roof. Damage to one is damage to all. The stability of one affects the stability of all, and therefore the proper maintenance and repair of one affects the others. This may have only a marginal effect on the owners of a semi, but in blocks of flats contributions have to be made to a mainten-ance fund. The annual charges – at least in one company's eyes – are linked to the following anticipated future expenses: new roof every 35 years; new drains every 50 years; new windows every 30 years; external redecoration every 7 years – and so on. This is quite apart from items like new lifts and maintenance of grounds. It is therefore necessary when conducting a survey of a flat to examine the lease to see what each owner is liable to pay for the upkeep of the building as a whole, to cross-question the managing agents on foreseeable charges, and to make some assessment of the state of the structure as a whole by looking in the roof space, checking for cracks in halls, staircases, basements and external walls. The external roof and upper storey walls should be examined with binoculars. All this is in addition to examining the flat itself in detail.

In the case of a terraced house or semi, inspection (so far as is possible) must be made of party walls, roof junctions, fire partition of roof spaces, common drives and paths; then let your solicitor deal with any problems of maintenance and repair arising, but be sure to establish the responsibilities. A common fault is that the roof space is not effectively isolated from its neighbours – the party wall must be fully complete up to the rafters and roof tiles so that no smoke can penetrate it. This is essential for safety against fire as well as for security against burglary.

And one final point – is the sound insulation adequate? Listen for the neighbours, and if possible ask them what they think!

TIMBER-FRAME CONTROVERSY

A controversial television documentary at the end of 1983 on timber-frame houses, which led to a tumble in share prices for leading house-builders, was itself attacked for being 'technically ill-informed and misleading'. The National House Building Council (NHBC), which guarantees the structure of most new houses for a period of 10 years and issues detailed technical instructions for the design and construction of dwellings, claimed that the 'World in Action' programme was 'alarmist'.

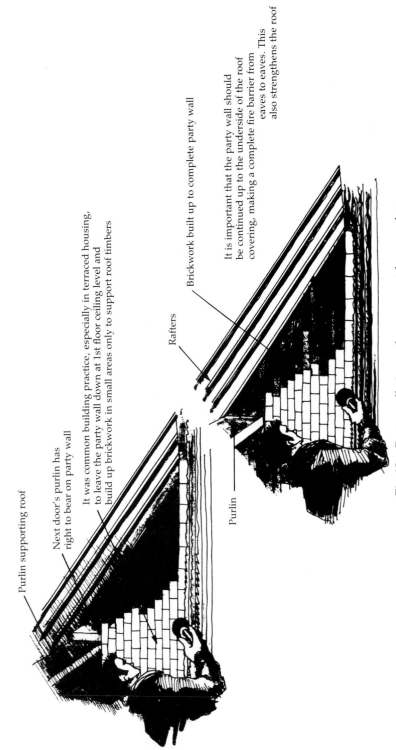

Purlin supporting roof

Next door's purlin has right to bear on party wall

It was common building practice, especially in terraced housing, to leave the party wall down at 1st floor ceiling level and build up brickwork in small areas only to support roof timbers

Brickwork built up to complete party wall

Rafters

It is important that the party wall should be continued up to the underside of the roof covering, making a complete fire barrier from eaves to eaves. This also strengthens the roof

Purlin

Fig 12   Party walls in roof space must be complete

The programme described faulty workmanship in a number of new timber-frame homes following a survey of more than a hundred building sites. It also revealed how easily bad workmanship could expose this type of house to the risk of damp and rot. Another criticism was that the homes were prone to fire, and it was revealed how one householder had accidentally set his property alight with a blow-torch.

The programme highlighted the importance of providing an effective 'vapour barrier' (usually a skin of plastic sheeting) behind the *internal* plasterboard surface – if moisture from inside the home seeped into the cavity it could rot the timber frame.

After the documentary was screened, the television station was besieged with calls from worried home-owners. The NHBC hit back by pointing out that its own design instructions were specifically introduced to compensate for mistakes on site and claimed that the documentary was misleading by being selective in its interviews and editing.

The Building Research Establishment was also quoted in the programme as saying:

> The main theoretical problem in timber frame con-struction is interstitial condensation. Builders should ensure that the 'vapour barrier' is intact, but in practice it never is. However, we monitor all reports of building failures in Britain and we have come across no evidence of interstitial condensation causing structural rot in practice.

The upshot of this was that a number of companies pulled out of the timber-frame house-building market and the proportion of houses built by this method had dropped from 24 to 17 per cent by the beginning of 1984, and is even less now.

For new home-owners, some builders have now given a 20-year guarantee against structural defects, but the NHBC has not followed suit. What of those stuck with a 10-year guarantee, or none at all? The fact is that the rotting process in timber can be long and slow, and may not be observed by the householder until a very advanced stage of decay has been reached.

Before the 10-year guarantee runs out therefore, a structural engineer should be asked to survey the house and to inspect the cavities with an endoscope which has a zoom eye-piece and a powerful light source in the tip. Alternatively/additionally, small sections of plasterboard should be removed at vulnerable points in the structure. This inspection should then be repeated every ten years so that remedial treatment can be undertaken at an early stage if rotting is detected.

USING TIMBER-FRAME

The use of timber frame in house building quadrupled in the 1970s and nearly half a million houses were built by this method. It is not surprising, therefore, that the main thrust of the anti timber-frame publicity has concentrated more on what could happen, rather than on what has actually happened.

Building by timber frame enables the factory-built super-structure of a house to be erected quickly – the average structure takes only 40 to 50 man-hours to erect ready for roofing. This reduces delays due to the weather and increases productivity, pay and builder's profit. On completing the timber structure and roof, the external walls are usually constructed of facing bricks, cement rendering on metal mesh, weather boarding or vertically hung clay tiles. The interior is covered with plasterboard which is then skimmed with plaster so that when the house is finished it is impossible to distinguish visually between this and the traditional structure where the load-bearing walls are solid brick or concrete blocks. In both structures the cavity in the walls between the inner and outer leaves contains insulation in the form of glass fibre or polystyrene.

It is, of course, quite easy to tell the difference by tapping the walls inside to see which are hollow, and in any case you will soon find out when you try to hang shelves, mirrors or pictures on the walls.

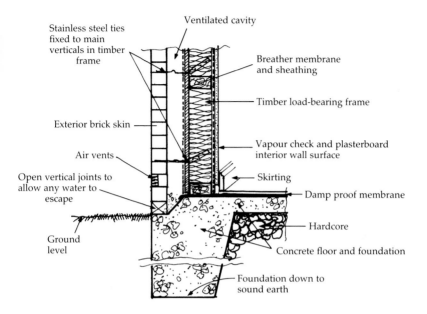

Stainless steel ties
fixed to main
verticals in timber
frame

Ventilated cavity

Breather membrane
and sheathing

Timber load-bearing frame

Exterior brick skin

Vapour check and plasterboard
interior wall surface

Air vents

Skirting

Open vertical joints to
allow any water to
escape

Damp proof membrane

Ground
level

Hardcore

Concrete floor and foundation

Foundation down to
sound earth

Problems arising from defects in workmanship or puncturing
of vapour membranes are not easy to detect, even for an
expert, without removing a section of the plasterboard

Fig 13   Section through wall of timber framed house

Condensation

Because the insulating characteristics of timber-frame
houses are so good they do give rise to the problem known
as 'interstitial condensation', as was revealed in the television documentary. Just as condensation will appear on a
window which is warm on one side and cold on the other,
so it will appear in the warm cavity of a house when it is
very cold outside. It will occur all the more if there is
residual moisture in the cavity arising from the building
process, or if it seeps in either from inside the house or from

some external source. There is no such thing in practice as a perfect vapour barrier, though this is not always as serious as it might appear. However, it is essential to predict where condensation will occur, and at what rate, so that steps can be taken in the design to reduce the risk of damage to a minimum. Urgent research is still needed to achieve this.

In North America, in areas where conditions are similar to this country, a survey showed that one per cent of houses were affected by damp, but rot was not found in any of these, and in the few years of experience here none of the faults so far reported are due to this cause. The reasons are that even a partly defective vapour barrier can still be effective, and preservative treatment to timber is carried out, following the disastrous effects of not doing so during the 1960s and early 1970s.

All the same, the potential exists, and it is only since September 1983 that new regulations on the treatment of timber-frame houses with preservatives have come into force. The requirements, which are mandatory, were published the previous December by the NHBC, and include measures to treat any timber which has to be cut during construction; however, their main aim is to ensure that the timber frame is kept dry in the moist British climate. Previously neither the Building Regulations nor the NHBC specifically legislated for this type of construction.

Fire Risk

So far as fire risks are concerned, this criticism has been a little overplayed and the Fire Research Station has stated categorically:

> Finally, we should emphasise again that the Fire Research Station has found no evidence that injury or death in fires is more likely in dwellings of timber-frame construction than in any other form of construction.

Whether the damage to the structure is likely to be greater can be left to your own judgement. It is some comfort to know that the insurance companies do not have any great concern on this score.

OFFICIAL REPORTS
Local Authorities Report

The local authorities also sounded a warning note. A major report published by the Association of Metropolitan Authorities (AMA) spoke of serious doubts about the long-term durability of this type of building. The report concluded that: 'Most of the advantages appear to benefit directly the builder or developer, whereas the consumer is left with a dwelling which must have some inherent risks, however small.' The report called for a continuing government-sponsored evaluation of timber-frame housing, longer-term guarantees, and voluntary limits by house-builders on the number of dwellings built by this method.

The AMA did recognise the advantages of timber-frame houses, namely that they are often quicker and, in some respects, cheaper to build; other benefits can include a higher standard of insulation as well as more economic use of on-site labour. However, the report concluded that because timber frame was import-dependent, its increasing use was damaging home-based brick and block industries. Potential defects and doubts about long-term durability were discussed at length.

The AMA also reported that defects from small design errors were more likely with timber frame than with traditional dwellings. Defects from bad workmanship were potentially higher, and serious accidental damage after occupation could arise because the occupier either would not know the house was timber-framed or would not be aware of its consequences – even attempting to hang a picture could cause potentially serious damage.

The Abbey National Building Society also called for stricter controls, especially in the form of new compulsory inspections on building sites to avoid risk of fire and condensation.

We are not saying that there is anything wrong with timber-frame homes if they are constructed properly. We would like to see closer control, and checks should be more stringent and more frequent. No-one is criticising the standard specifications laid down – if they are followed. We are simply questioning whether building operatives are doing the job properly and whether quality control is high enough. We would like to see more careful quality control and we will continue to press for it.

They also made a good point, that all timber-frame houses should be formally recorded as such either by the NHBC or on the title deeds, 'so that people realise they are living in a timber-frame house and can take professional advice when making alterations'.

The last point is important since we have become used to structural walls being of solid construction, and normally it would not occur to a DIY or small builder carrying out alterations that walls could be otherwise.

BRE Report

Shortly after this the Building Research Establishment (BRE) published its own report called 'Timber-frame housing: a technical appraisal' which found that there was no evidence of any more problems, or greater risk of major defects due to deficiencies in design or workmanship, than in traditionally constructed houses.

After two years of research, the BRE found no evidence of rot due to condensation, although the report warned that the trend towards increased thermal insulation and reduced ventilation *might* increase the risk of condensation within a timber-framed structure. In an official statement, the BRE said that the few cases of rot it knew about were in every case directly attributable to rising damp or to rain penetration:

A vapour barrier is installed to resist the passage through the structure, from the interior of the dwelling, of water vapour which might otherwise condense and create

Timber frames – vulnerable to rain during construction

conditions of damp. There is some evidence that transitory dampness can occur, possibly due to this condensation, in a small number of dwellings, but there is no evidence that it has led to rot.

It also commented that the Building Regulations required installation of cavity barriers to limit fire spread and a completely fire-resistant lining to the inside of the dwelling.

NHBC View

Reassurance for the owners of timber-frame homes came from the director-general of the NHBC, who argued:

If we really believed it was risky we would have a financial interest against timber-frame being built. It makes no difference to our income whether it is timber-frame or brick and block. If we believed it would have an adverse effect on claims, we would discourage people from buying timber-frame. We are not doing that; with our new standards they represent as good a risk as any house.

However, as the NHBC risk is limited to 10 years and faults cannot be detected easily in the early stages, that assurance should surely be backed by an increase in the period of guarantee to, say, 25 years. Personally I would also like to see a substantial increase in the overhang of eaves, such as one sees in Canada, Australia and Austria, which protects the outer walls – particularly on single-storey houses – and makes gutter maintenance easier. Without these two measures, and especially as structural engineers are not involved in the inspection of buildings on the building site, one is left with a feeling of disquiet with regard to the long-term integrity of structures using sealed-in timber components.

If you already have a timber-frame house, however, do not be alarmed! Simply take the precaution of having a structural survey carried out before the 10-year guarantee expires, and at 10-yearly intervals thereafter.

6 · Drainage, Water, Gas and Electrical Services

Drains and Septic Tanks · Water, Gas and Heating
Electrical Services

DRAINS AND SEPTIC TANKS
Sewers

In order for a house to be maintained in a healthy state it is necessary to provide a means whereby soil and waste water can be quickly and inoffensively removed from the property. Additionally, rainwater from roofs and pavements needs to be controlled and removed in order to provide a clean access and to avoid saturating the subsoil, which could lead to damp and foundation problems.

In urban areas, water is removed by means of continuous pipes or drains below ground level. The term 'drain' refers to a single house, whereas 'sewer' refers to a collective system serving more than one property. Private sewers are the responsibility of the individual owner, whereas public sewers are the responsibility of the local authority. It is therefore essential to know which drains are the house-holder's responsibility, even if they run across someone else's land; and which private sewers are 'shared', and the point at which the local authority public sewer becomes

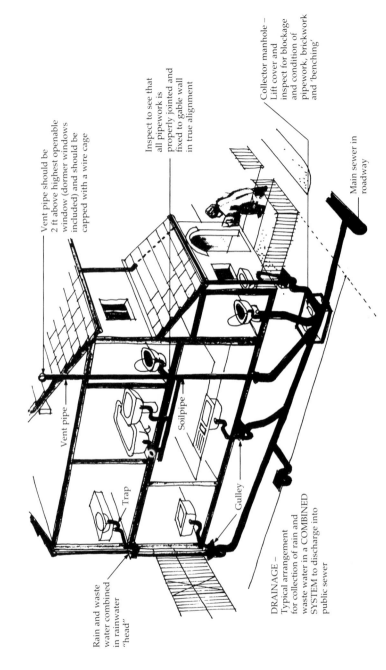

Vent pipe should be 2 ft above highest openable window (dormer windows included) and should be capped with a wire cage

Inspect to see that all pipework is properly jointed and fixed to gable wall in true alignment

Collector manhole – Lift cover and inspect for blockage and condition of pipework, brickwork and 'benching'

Main sewer in roadway

Vent pipe

Trap

Soilpipe

Gulley

Rain and waste water combined in rainwater "head"

DRAINAGE – Typical arrangement for collection of rain and waste water in a COMBINED SYSTEM to discharge into public sewer

Fig 14   Waste water and drains

responsible. The deeds, the solicitor and the local building inspector will confirm the position.

Cess Pools and Septic Tanks

In rural areas the house drains, where they are not connected to sewers, are directed into enclosed tanks called cess pools or into septic tanks.

A cess pool has to be airtight, and installed where it can be readily emptied by pumps and motor tankers from time to time.

A septic tank is an open system and depends on being sited where it can eventually discharge into a natural watercourse or soakaway. By bacteriological process, human waste is reduced to a purified liquid suitable for

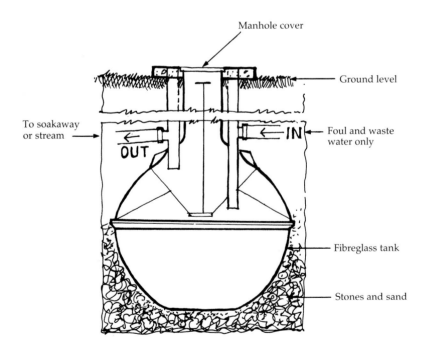

Fig 15   Septic tank

discharge. It is highly desirable for economic and functional reasons that rainwater discharges should not enter either cess pools or septic tanks, but should run into streams, ditches, collecting tanks or soakaways.

Drains

There are two basic systems of drains; the 'separate' system whereby foul waste water is kept entirely separate from rainwater, and the combined system where they run together in the same pipe. Most local authorities insist on separate systems to reduce the volume intake at sewage

Leaking W.C. pipe affects ceiling below

A fine roof, but valley gutters are difficult to maintain

works, since rainwater can be discharged into the nearest watercourse without treatment.

Most drains and sewers perform their task by gravity flow, and to ensure that the pipes are self-cleansing they should flow at about 1·5 metres per second. If they flow too slowly or too fast, deposits can be left behind. The pipes must, by law, be not less than 100mm (4in) in diameter and be made of non-absorbent, non-corrodable material, be bedded firmly, have watertight joints and run in straight lines with manholes placed over changes in direction.

No drain should pass under a building, but where this is unavoidable it must be specially protected by encasing in concrete and supported against settlement where it passes through a wall or foundation.

Drains should be kept clear of trees to avoid damage by roots. All manholes must have covers which give access for clearing blockages, and which must be of adequate strength to take pedestrian traffic or, in the case of driveways,

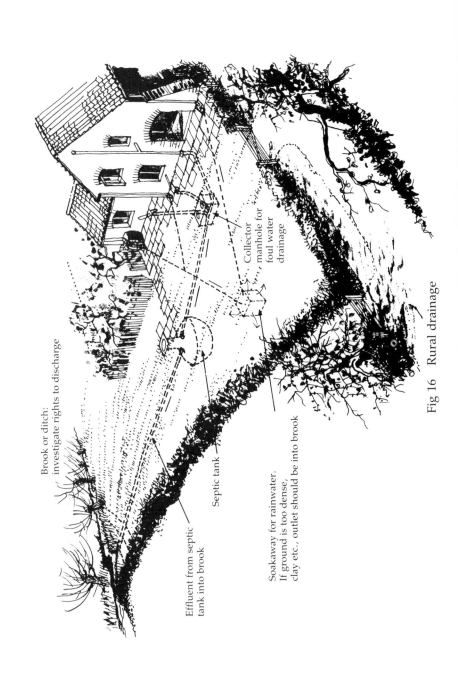

Brook or ditch:
investigate rights to discharge

Collector
manhole for
foul water
drainage

Septic tank

Effluent from septic
tank into brook

Soakaway for rainwater.
If ground is too dense,
clay etc., outlet should be into brook

Fig 16   Rural drainage

vehicles. Inside the manholes the open channels must be set in fine mortar or concrete 'benching', with steep falls and smooth finishes.

All drains should be ventilated to avoid the build-up of sewer gas. This is usually achieved by extending the main house downpipe above the roof (and covering it with a bird grill). Ends of branches that make a connection directly into manholes are called gullies, and these are all fitted with 'U' or 'S' traps to form a water seal. These gullies *and* traps should be firmly bedded in concrete and kept clean. They require flushing at least twice a year.

Gutters and Downpipes

So far as rainwater is concerned, this should discharge cleanly from the roof into an eaves gutter preferably 150mm (6in) in diameter, though 100mm (4in) is acceptable on short runs. In heavy rain it should not overshoot the gutter. The gutter is supported at frequent intervals on brackets which can be raised or lowered to determine its 'fall', and gutters must run to a good fall and should be cleaned at least annually to free them of leaves and mud; they must not sag between brackets. They discharge into downpipes and thence into gullies, traps and drains. Gutters and down-pipes, once made of cast iron, are now nearly always of PVC, and none the worse for that except that they need more frequent supports.

The essence of a good drainage system, be it for foul or rainwater, lies in clean, straight runs, adequately sized pipes, good falls, carefully made joints and avoidance of leakage onto the building fabric at every point of contact.

Soakaways

Where rainwater 'soakaways' are used, they should be at least 5m (16ft 6in) from the foundations, and consist of an excavated pit not less than a 1m cube filled with gravel and surrounded by silt, sand and gravel. The pit should be covered with paving to avoid soil seeping into it.

WATER, GAS AND HEATING SERVICES
Water Mains

Apart from the small number of houses in rural areas where water is obtained from a suitable private source like a spring, mountain stream or well, most water is provided through pipes which are called 'mains'. The pressure of water in the mains is based on the fire-fighting requirements of a locality. This pressure is maintained by means of water towers and gravity, or by booster pumping stations. The mains are buried about one metre below ground level so they do not freeze up, and outside each house they are tapped by a connecting pipe fitted with a stop-cock. From there on, within the boundary of the property, it becomes the owner's responsibility.

This cold water supply pipe is usually 15mm (½in) in diameter (internal dimension) and enters the house below ground level to a further stop-cock inside the house, often near the kitchen sink. It then becomes the 'rising main' to a storage tank in the roof space. Some water boards insist that all cold water taps in the house are taken from the rising main; others insist that only the kitchen tap is taken from the main and that all others are fed from the roof tank. This is an obnoxious requirement designed to suit the water board's storage calculations and not the consumer's wishes; you can determine which system is installed by turning on each tap in turn and putting your thumb over the outlet. If you can stop the flow fairly easily it is the latter. If you can't, then you have mains pressure from the rising main.

Mains pipes should be made of plastic or copper. If they are lead or iron they are old and will have to be replaced before long. If the water is hard the pipes will almost certainly be reduced in internal diameter by scale and the pressure will be reduced. Test the kitchen cold tap fully opened to see what the flow and pressure is like. It should be vigorous, not sluggish.

According to the water authorities, most water from the mains is safe to drink, but in fact some 2·5 million people in this country are drinking sub-standard water. The two main causes are lead and nitrates which can bring about debility, heart weakness and cancer. The soft and acid water areas of Scotland and north-west England are most at risk from lead, and the East Anglian and Staffordshire areas from nitrates. Tap water also contains varying amounts of rust, grit and silt.

There are many different water filters and softeners on the market, but you should take nothing for granted, so consult the local water authority before using any of these devices. And remember, in accordance with the Public Health Act 1936, amended in 1961, it is the duty of every water authority to ensure that all supplies are clean, clear, unodorous, wholesome and palatable! The water boards are always prepared to discuss pressure and purity, but whether they will do anything about it is another matter, and the effects of privatisation have yet to be seen.

Storage Tanks

The water cistern will be in the roof space or in a high cupboard and should be of an approved plastic construction, clean, strong and with the seal of approval of the National

Well insulated and well supported roof storage tank – untidy plumbing and lagging, but acceptable

Water Council. It should have a readily removable cover which fits closely without being airtight, and should be protected against frost by insulating material. The inlet pipe, or rising main, enters at the top of the tank to a ball-valve. The outlet should be 100mm (4in) from the bottom of the tank, to be free of sediment. A 20mm (¾in) overflow pipe from near the top of the tank should take water by gravity (with a fall of 1 in 10 minimum) to 150mm (6in) or so beyond the outer walls of the house where its discharge will be safe and visible. The overflow should be some 50mm (2in) above the cistern water level. For the average property, the cistern should have a capacity of 230 litres (50 gallons).

Gas

Natural gas contains up to 95 per cent methane, a gas with a high calorific value which requires ten times its own volume of air for complete combustion. It is therefore essential that any room where gas is used must be adequately supplied with air, and must have an adequate flue to discharge the burnt gases, which are toxic.

The service pipe from the Gas Board mains to the property must be laid by the Gas Board or by their nominee. This pipe is usually a 25mm (1in) diameter *steel* pipe, wrapped with special tape to protect it from rusting, and buried to protect it from frost. It should be laid to a fall with a drain cock to release condensation in the pipe. The pipe must not pass through the foundations and should enter the external wall of the house through a sleeve which permits movement, and then lead to a meter which controls the volume and pressure. The meter and service pipe should not touch or be close to any electrical conduit or apparatus.

Installation pipes from the meter should be of steel or copper and should be surface-mounted and away from electrical services and appliances. All pipes should be bracketed to avoid accidental damage.

Gas leakages can be detected by smell or by instruments.

Any evidence of leakage should be dealt with immediately by turning off the supply at the meter stop-cock and calling the Gas Board. Only the Gas Board or a CORGI (Confederation for the Registration of Gas Installers) registered contractor may carry out any work at all on gas service pipes or equipment.

Heating

Remember this – official figures show that two million houses in England alone are inadequately heated. So in carrying out your survey, try to find the answers to the following questions:

What kind of heating is installed?
Does it operate efficiently and keep the house warm in winter?
How old is it and what condition is it in? Is it safe?
What controls are there, and do they work?
Can you afford the running costs and maintenance costs?
When was it last serviced, by whom, and what service agreements or guarantees exist?
Is it what you want anyway?

If there is an open fire, you must have a coal bunker of reasonable size at hand, and there must be a coal merchant willing to deliver good quality coal, or smokeless fuel if it is a smokeless zone. Check! There must be a clean and efficient way of disposing of the ash. There must be adequate ventilation into the room, and the flue must be in good condition and have a good draught, with no susceptibility to down-draught. You can try burning paper and wood in the grate, and from its appearance you can usually tell whether the fireplace is in general use or not. Ask when the chimney was last swept and by whom.

If gas fires are fitted into chimney flues, and if the Gas Board has serviced the appliances recently, you can be reasonably satisfied that the installations are safe. Otherwise beware of ill-fitted appliances, blocked flues and badly

If it looks wrong . . . apart from the damage to the lower roof and the unsightliness, the fumes from the boiler are discharging at eaves level and may enter the roof space

Discharge from boiler is direct and well above roof level

maintained heaters – all can cause lethal fumes. And remember, flues should *not* be interconnected with any other room. Once again, good ventilation *into* the room is essential.

Central heating boilers should only be fitted to a flue that has been lined with a stainless steel flexible liner of about 150mm (6in) diameter. Boiler size depends upon the sum of all the room requirements plus an allowance for domestic hot water, plus a little to spare. Both free-standing and wall-mounted gas boilers come in conventional chimney flue versions, or in a balanced flue version, where a combined terminal on an outside wall provides a fresh air inlet and an exhaust gas outlet.

Even if appliances appear to be in good order, allow for the cost of immediate testing and servicing by the Gas Board, CORGI registered contractor or, in the case of oil, the oil company's nominee, as soon as you move in.

If electric night storage heaters are installed, check that they are included in the sale, as well as any electric or gas fires. Do not assume that storage heaters can operate satisfactorily without supplementation by fires or radiators of one sort or another – there is no substitute for instant heat when and where you want it. Check that the wiring is new and in good condition, and immediately on occupation ask the Electricity Board to safety-check the whole installation – appliances and wiring. Allow for this check in your costs.

There is no ideal system of central heating, and life would be so much simpler if there were. But each of us is different, and our needs vary according to the time of day and what we are doing. In a house, however, all calculations are based on assumptions of 'heat loss' through walls, windows, roof, floors, and through draught and ventilation. This heat loss depends also on the temperature outside (the lower it is, the more heat you lose) and the temperature you require inside (the higher it is, the more you lose). It also depends on the sun – a south-facing window will add more heat than it loses, winter or summer, though not always when you want it.

Boilers have other uses – but these must not affect the flow of air required for combustion

Walls should have plastic or metal sleeves through which pipes can pass, to allow for expansion

Central heating systems circulate either hot water or warm air throughout the house, and can also provide domestic hot water. In a warm-air system, air is heated by gas, electricity, oil or solid fuel and is then circulated through large ducts to all parts of the house. The domestic hot water is usually provided from a separate boiler or electric immersion heater fitted to the hot water cylinder.

In a hot water radiator system, water is heated by a gas, oil or solid fuel boiler and circulated through pipes and radiators. Domestic hot water may be supplied in two ways, 'directly' or 'indirectly'. A direct system has only one water circuit which supplies both the taps and the radiators. Each time hot water is drawn from the taps the whole system has to be topped up with cold water from the storage tank. This frequent introduction of new water is a major disadvantage, as scaling occurs when water is heated to 71°C (160°F). Because of this, the system is rarely used now, but it does still exist in some older houses.

The more normal 'indirect' system has two water circuits: a primary circuit which is heated in the boiler and then circulates to a heat-exchange unit inside the hot water cylinder before returning to the boiler to be reheated; and a second circuit which runs from the boiler to the radiators. The two circuits are self-contained and lose no water other than by leaks and evaporation, so no scaling occurs after the initial heating of the water. The hot water cylinder supplies the domestic hot water to the taps. When hot water is drawn from the taps, new cold water is fed into the cylinder from the cold storage tank above. A small 'balance' tank is provided in the roof space for topping up the evaporation losses in the radiator circuits. This is fitted with a ball valve inlet, an outlet, an overflow, and, hooked over it, an expansion pipe. One rôle of this pipe is to provide an unobstructed path for water in the cylinder to expand as it is heated. It follows that it also ensures that there is no possibility of the cylinder exploding due to pressure or overheating. Its main function, however, is to ensure that the system rids itself of unwanted air. Occasionally air becomes trapped in radiators and cannot escape to reach

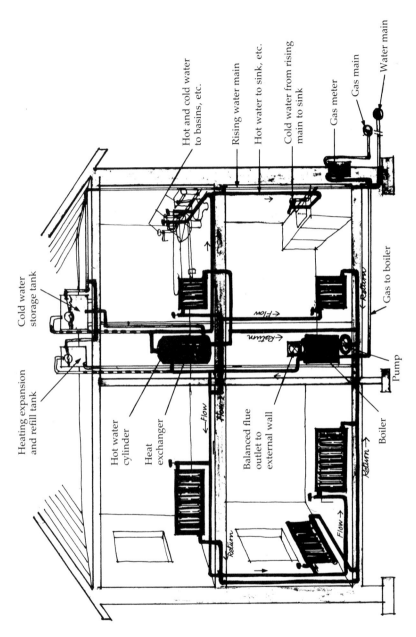

Cold water
storage tank

Heating expansion
and refill tank

Hot water
cylinder

Heat
exchanger

Balanced flue
outlet to
external wall

Hot and cold water
to basins, etc.

Rising water main

Hot water to sink, etc.

Cold water from rising
main to sink

Gas meter

Gas main

Water main

Gas to boiler

Pump

Boiler

Flow

Return

Return

Flow

Return

Flow

Return

Flow

Fig 17   Central heating – hot and cold water supply

the expansion/vent pipe. That is why each radiator is fitted with a 'bleed' valve which can be opened with a small key – an essential tool in every house with central heating radiators.

You can identify a 'direct' system by examining the boiler. If there are only two pipes leading to/from the boiler, it is direct. 'Indirect' has four pipes, though sometimes it has only three, when the balance tank in the roof is combined with the storage tank, or when an ancient 'primatic' cylinder has been fitted. The best systems have four pipes plus a balance tank and hot water cylinder. Anything less is out of date and needs changing.

In some heating systems the water circulates naturally; hot water rising from the boiler and returning to it by force of gravity when it is cooler. However, most systems now use a pump, which is usually next to the boiler.

As the prospective purchaser, you must decide whether you prefer gas, oil or solid fuel, and if you are not satisfied with what is there, ask the vendor if alternatives are available or not, and check these afterwards. Generally speaking it only pays to change a system when it has reached the end of its economic life – usually 20 years.

Controls are vital. Every radiator should have an adjustable 'lock shield' valve, a thermostatic (or on/off) valve, and a valve for 'bleeding'. These should be free of leaks and rust, and circulating pipes should be neatly and securely fixed. Every boiler should have an efficient thermostat to govern its output. Every installation should be fitted with an expansion pipe which provides a safety discharge over the top of the balance tank or cold water feed tank in the roof space; a safety blow-off valve near the boiler; drainage cocks for emptying the system conveniently; a hot-water thermostat and a room thermostat.

Solid fuel systems require facilities for fuel storage and ash disposal, and will need attention at frequent intervals. Oil and gas systems are similar to each other, but oil requires a large storage tank and a reliable delivery service.

Finally, all systems require frost-stats to prevent freeze-ups, and numerous isolating stop-cocks. All require annual servicing by skilled tradesmen, and all except electric heaters need an adequate air supply for combustion, and they produce toxic gases which must be safely dispersed to the outside air.

ELECTRICAL SERVICES

Official figures show that one million houses in England alone require re-wiring. Be warned!

Mains Cables

Domestic properties are supplied with electricity by means of two wires, one termed the 'phase wire', the other the 'neutral'. The phase wire is connected to one of the three phase wires forming part of the Electricity Board's main supply (3 phase and 1 neutral). The connections are sealed joints and only the Electricity Board may make these joints and provide the two service wires to each house, where they terminate in a sealed, fused container. These service lines may be buried (where they should be covered by clay tiles) or carried by overhead cables attached to insulators secured to poles. The line should be capable of at least a 60 amp supply and possibly up to 100 amp for a large property or heavy user.

From the sealed fused container located inside the house, 'tails' are taken to the consumer control switch, past a main fuse to the consumer's distribution unit with 6, 8 or 10 connecting points and fuses. From these connecting points circuit wires are fed to the various parts of the property where outlets are required.

To protect each line, fuses of relevant capacity are incorporated in the positive line of the circuit before it leaves the consumer unit. It is vital that throughout the installation all positive lines are fused. Mistakes between positive and neutral fusing are critical and could be fatal, which is why it is vital that work on the electrical circuits should only be carried out by the Electricity Board or by an NICEIC (National Inspection Council for Electrical Installation Con-

Service meters should be fixed in a box to the outside of the house, where they are visible

tracting) registered contractor. And this is why any new owner is strongly advised to have at least a safety inspection of the system carried out immediately on moving in. Allow for this modest cost in addition to your own survey.

All wiring should be in pvc-covered cable, and all outlets should be modern 13 amp and switched. Any installation more than 25 years old will need some renewal, as well as new sockets and a new consumer unit incorporating an earth-linkage trip safety device. The Electricity Board will tell you what you need to bring the installation up to scratch. For a new house, a certificate of acceptance by the Electricity Board should be insisted upon. Apparatus such as immersion heaters, boilers, electric cookers and so on require a separate supply with direct entry cables (no plugs) into fused sockets. Door bells and shavers etc require a separate fused supply through a transformer.

All sockets, conduits and cables should be well clear of gas lines and points, and for safety no electrical socket should be reachable from a sink or washbasin with taps, to avoid wet hands touching plugs or switches.

Power circuits are now in ring mains, where the cable is in a continuous loop starting and finishing at the consumer unit. This makes it easier to add additional sockets, which are likely to cost in excess of £30 per point. Check the number and position of points and allow for your additional requirements; check the lighting points and allow for extras and alterations in your costs.

Burglar Alarm Systems

If you inherit one of these, it must be covered by a service agreement or it is unreliable. These systems require frequent attention and expense, and even the most up-to-date can be a nuisance to neighbours. The latest excuse offered by one firm whose recently installed system woke the neighbourhood at 2am whilst the owners were away, was that spiders were crawling across the sensor, or moths were flying across it!

Much of the deterrent value of the installation lies in having a box on the wall outside the house, but for the rest it is a matter of personal inclination. Good external lighting with heat sensors is a different matter, and one to be commended – the Electricity Board or an NICEIC contractor will fit these for you. And if you have double locks fitted to windows and doors, plus locks on internal doors, you have first class security. If you want to install a burglar alarm, however, ask the police which company they recommend; if you inherit one, then examine the service agreement carefully to see what the charges are, what it covers and what notice is required if you wish to terminate it.

Telephones

You will know your own requirements for telephones, so check with the vendor and British Telecom what system you are inheriting and whether there are any problems in that area. British Telecom will give you an estimate of the cost of any changes you require. It is usual nowadays to have the plug-in 'jack' system installed in a number of locations to provide flexibility and greater choice of instruments.

7 · Detailed Sequence and Method of Survey

Equipment and Documents · Sequence of Inspection
Internal Inspection · External Inspection · Fences,
Drives and Vegetation · Measurement of house and
boundaries · Report and Negotiation

EQUIPMENT AND DOCUMENTS
Equipment

Large measuring tape in feet and metres (50ft/15·2m)

Small measuring tape in feet and metres (6-9ft/1·8-2·7m)

Small pocket screwdriver

Two large screwdrivers

Garden spade

Large torch

Plumb line

Pocket level

Ladder and/or steps to gain access to the roof space (usually
the vendor will provide this)

Binoculars

Camera with flash attachment

Clipboard and pencil

The above is what you will need, and if possible buy, borrow or hire a moisture meter from a DIY shop. One maker is Protimeter Ltd of Marlow, Bucks SL7 1LX, who will also provide advice, information and analysis of damp plaster, wallpaper, and so on.

Dress

Wear overalls or old clothes, and carry a piece of rag.

Documents

Obtain from your solicitor copies of the Land Registry Plan and the Ownership and Charges Register, showing the land, boundaries, restrictive covenants, etc. Usually the plan gives dimensions and the ownership of hedges and fences, though these are sometimes defined in writing. If the land is not so far 'registered' (you solicitor will tell you) then the Abstract of Title and Deeds will suffice.

Read every word and study the plans, before and after your survey, and if you do not understand any point, or if what you see or have seen is at variance with what is set down in the documents, then it is VITAL that you consult your solicitor before exchanging contracts.

In the documents there will be covenants and agreements which show your obligations – they usually relate to fences and use of the property, but they may also restrict you in extending or altering the property, define the colour of the front door, forbid you to keep a caravan or boat in the drive, and so on. Particularly note if anyone else has a right over your land in respect of paths, drives, drains, mains services, mining for minerals, use of streams or beds of streams etc, and note whether your external drains and mains services cross anyone else's land. Take nothing for granted. Note, inspect and question!

Obtain from your solicitor or the vendor *copies* of all guarantees such as those for damp-proofing, wood treatment, new windows, roofs etc. Read every line carefully – they will be teeming with exclusions, and if the firms have gone out of business or the guarantees are non-transferable, they are useless. If it is a newish house, then read the NHBC warranty thoroughly.

Finally, take with you a spare copy of the 'particulars' from the estate agent, to check his details line by line, measure by measure, as these are nearly always inaccurate or incomplete.

Weather and Time

If it is a wet day or it has recently been raining, so much the better for showing up leaks and dampness. If there has been a prolonged spell of dry weather, leaks and damp are more difficult to detect and you should be doubly suspicious of stains, water marks and white crystals if you see them. Remember that the vendor may not wish to have you around the house at all, so try to agree a mutually convenient time, starting at, say, 9am or 2pm, which will allow at least three daylight hours for the survey. Ask the vendor about access to the roof space or spaces, and ask if all the keys to rooms, cupboards, garages, sheds etc, might be made available. Request also that the past year's water, gas and electricity bills, and the service agreements for boilers, security alarms etc, be available for your inspection, if you do not already have them.

SEQUENCE OF INSPECTION

On arrival, don't waste time. Ask the vendor if you can defer discussion until you've completed the survey, so that all matters arising can be dealt with at one go. You will be reasonably familiar with the layout of the house, and you can explain to the vendor that you will be working in the following sequence:

1 Preliminary external inspection
2 Internal roof space
3 Rooms on upper floor(s)
4 Rooms on ground floor

Steel S plates indicate use of ties to secure porch to main building

5 Cellars, attached garages etc
6 Detailed external inspection
7 Detached garages, sheds, greenhouses
8 External services – manholes, drains, water, electricity, gas, TV aerials, telephone wires etc
9 Fences, hedges, gates, drives, paving, paths, shrubs and trees
10 Measurement of land boundaries, external measurement of house and outbuildings

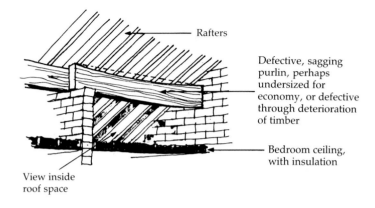

Rafters

Defective, sagging purlin, perhaps undersized for economy, or defective through deterioration of timber

Bedroom ceiling, with insulation

View inside roof space

When seen from outside, indications are wavy ridge, depression in general roof slope, slates or tiles lying unevenly

Fig 18　Fault in roof structural timbers

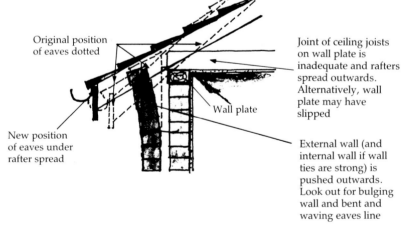

Original position of eaves dotted

Joint of ceiling joists on wall plate is inadequate and rafters spread outwards. Alternatively, wall plate may have slipped

Wall plate

New position of eaves under rafter spread

External wall (and internal wall if wall ties are strong) is pushed outwards. Look out for bulging wall and bent and waving eaves line

Fig 19　Fault due to spreading of roof span

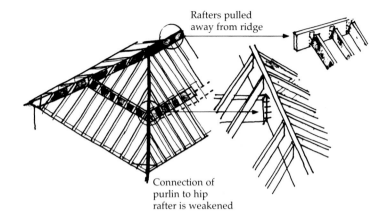

Rafters pulled away from ridge

Connection of purlin to hip rafter is weakened

Members carefully cut and fixed together to form a strong, stable roof become separated by stress from instability in foundations, exceptionally strong winds, etc., or defective joints and fungal decay

Look carefully in roof spaces for separation of 'joined' timbers

Fig 20   Separation of timbers in roof structure

Keep in the forefront of your mind the question – is it structurally sound? You are looking especially for cracks in walls, bulging or leaning walls and chimney breasts; damp, and rotting or infested wood; signs of movement, or subsidence; bulging or sagging floors and ceilings; broken, soft or hollow plaster; blocked or inadequate drains; adequate and safe water, gas and electrical services. Be especially suspicious of alterations and additions to the original building. Particularly note any steel plates (circular, S-shaped, X-shaped or rectangular) which have been fixed to the walls. These usually indicate the presence of steel tie-rods used to hold a defective structure together. If you spot these, stop your inspection and call in a structural engineer.

Secondly, you are looking out for minor defects which

will cost you time and money – plumbing, heating, redecoration, bathroom and kitchen fittings, replacement windows, floor finishes, insulation etc.

Finally, you are looking to see that you are getting value for money, and getting what you are paying for – area of land, size of rooms, and (dare I say it?) good neighbours. Watch out for the caravans, motorbikes, shared drives, boat enthusiasts and the feckless!

Now, back to the survey in detail.

Preliminary External Inspection

As you walk around the outside, look for any defects which may reflect themselves internally. You can make a more thorough examination later, but draw a quick plan and mark on it any large cracks or bulges, especially at eaves level, which could indicate that the roof structure is pushing outwards. Look at the gutters and downpipes for damp patches, and look out for water marks and white salts. Inspect the dpc 150mm (6in) above ground level – a series of holes just above the dpc at 150mm intervals will indicate that a chemical dpc has been added. Bear in mind the age of the house, but note any oddities such as signs of recent building work, alterations to chimneys (sketch the position of all chimneys), or redecoration in patches which might indicate a 'cover-up'. Inspect these closely inside, and later outside. Photograph any peculiarities.

For timber-frame houses, flats and party walls, see Chapter 5.

Internal Roof Space

Do not climb a ladder or stepladder until you are sure it is high enough and stable – this applies particularly to getting into the roof space. And remember you have to get down again, so test it first.

If there is a light in the roof space, good – but you will still need your torch.

As you climb through the trap door look carefully at the

Roof timbers and wall plate – patterns of fungal decay and rain penetration

Load-bearing walls supporting roof structure must be continuous down to the foundations

frame and joists around the opening – this is a common place for woodworm. Look for the tell-tale holes and prod hard with your small, sharp screwdriver to test the wood. Do the same at intervals throughout the roof on occasional joists, rafters, purlins and trusses – and you must get down on your knees to reach right to the eaves and wall-plates. Note whether there is adequate ventilation. If not, be even more suspicious.

It is safe to move about by treading on the joists, but do not on any account tread on the plasterboard as it will give way. Be careful to avoid walking on, or tripping over, electric cables. Search (and smell) for dry rot and wet rot; look for wood splits and twists, and inadequate joints and supports. Stop and take a good look at the main structure – the tiles, battens, rafters, purlins, beams, wall-plates, trusses, joints. Check that each transfers its load securely to the one below, and hence onto the walls. And if the roof is made up of a series of roof trusses, these should all be joined up by timbers running the length of the roof to prevent a 'domino' kind of collapse.

Note on a plan which internal walls take the structural load. Are there any twisted or precarious joints? Any sagging, wet or damaged timbers? If in any doubt, photograph using flash. If the house is semi-detached or terraced, the party walls *must* continue up through the roof space to form a fire and smoke barrier between the properties (see Chapter 5). Any flues must be smoke and fire proof. Furthermore, chimney walls and all internal structural walls visible in the roof space and in the rooms below *must* be continuous down to the foundations. Beware of any chimney breast or wall which has been removed or partly removed in any room at any level. Sketch, make notes, and check them as you go down.

Make a note of the insulation, the thickness (not less than 100mm/4in) and whether is is complete and well fitted. Are the roof tank, the 'balance' tank and the plumbing adequately insulated? Examine the water tank, removing the cover: is it old, rusty, made of metal? Are the joints, ball valves and pipes newish? Are they correctly positioned? Is there one tank, or two? This will help you identify the kind of central heating system (if there is one). Does the 'expansion' pipe hook over the tank and is it free and unobstructed (see Chapter 6)?

Is the roof space clean and clear of rubbish? What is the condition of the electrical wiring?

Before you leave the roof space, sit down (on a joist) and write out your notes in full; have a last look round. Basically ask yourself, is the structure sound? Is is standing up to its job? Are there signs of rot, infestation or damp? Is it well ventilated? Has it been looked after and well maintained? If in doubt you will need to consult a builder later with your photographs or, in the case of rot or infestation, to ask for a wood treatment survey.

Rooms on the Upper Floors

You'll probably need to wash your hands, so start your survey on the upper floor, in the bathroom; as you wash, check the water pressure in the taps, examine the fittings, lift the carpet in the corners and check the floorboards for damp and woodworm – and inspect the plumbing and heating as far as you are able (see Chapter 6). Tap the tiling at intervals to see if it is hollow, and make a note of any work that you would need to carry out, guessing what it would cost to the nearest £100. Take the measurements and make a sketch.

From the bathroom, work round in one direction, say clockwise, inspecting each room in turn and returning finally to the bathroom. Check all built-in cupboards, doors and door furniture; windows (inside and out) and sills (inside and out); walls, skirtings and architraves; picture rails and ceilings; electrical outlets and lighting; radiators and valves; finally plumbing and floors (where the carpet can be lifted). You are searching for damp and woodworm, for lack of maintenance, and for usability and quality, or lack of it. Observe, measure, sketch, test by tapping, prodding with your screwdriver where it looks suspicious. Do not leave a room until you have completed your notes and sketches, and remember to pay attention to any damp or cracks around the chimney breasts.

Remember, too, to check the external defects you may have noticed on your preliminary external inspection. If there is an internal crack greater than 1mm, check this on the outside of the house later. If it runs right through, then you need a builder to inspect it for you; if it is greater than 2mm, a structural engineer. Poke around any plumbing, lift any loose floorboards and inspect the joists, using your screwdriver and torch. Decide on the condition of the windows, doors, decoration and fittings. Put down an expenditure figure for each repair (again to the nearest £100).

Inspect the hot water cylinder and pipework carefully. Are they lagged? Are they new or newish? Look for signs of corrosion, leakage or stains on tank or floor. Check valves and controls. Do they all look right? Is an immersion heater fitted? Is the wiring in good condition? – it should run directly into a switch and fuse (no plugs and sockets!). Anything suspicious? If in doubt, assume some expenditure will be required and put down a figure. Don't worry if it isn't accurate. The figures will surprisingly even themselves out over all.

Remember your load-bearing walls and chimneys from the roof inspection? Then make sure you know which they are and check them to see they have not been removed or weakened. If they have, then a structural engineer must be asked to advise. Note that a load-bearing wall might be removed or weakened without causing *immediate* collapse, but it is still unsafe and liable to collapse if any strain is imposed on it.

In each room, bounce on your heels in each corner and in the centre. The floor should be firm, level and noiseless. If not, then the cause may be ill-fitting boards or defective joists, which must be inspected by lifting a floorboard here and there if it is at all possible.

Check the ventilation in each room, particularly if there are gas or coal fires.

Damp in the upper parts of these rooms will almost certainly be from roof defects and/or gutters. Damp at floor level will nearly always be due to plumbing and heating pipe leaks. Check all taps, showers, baths and waste pipes for efficiency by running the water full on, and test the WC by putting a piece of loo paper in the pan and flushing it. Does it clear first time?

Before finishing each room, just spend a minute thinking about your furniture and how it will fit in. Are there any snags regarding wall space, radiators, electric sockets, lighting, windows? Are the windows safe for children? Are the room heights greater than 7ft 6in (2·3m)? Will you need more washbasins or a shower, and can these be easily installed?

Finally, check the upper hall and then the staircase, remembering to go under the stairs as well, which is a weak point for woodworm and damp. Shake the stair banisters and rail – are they loose? Are they safe? Are the stairs in good, sound condition? Bounce your heels on them. If the staircase is suffering from poor design or bad workmanship, from wood rot or heavy infestation by woodworm, if it has loose joists or suffers separation from the wall – then you can mark down a major defect, as it will probably require complete renewal.

Rooms on the Ground Floor

Repeat the process as defined for the upper floors, inspecting each room in a convenient order, but with three important additions: inspect for rising damp; check the security of the windows and doors; and finally check the meters, valves and fuses etc, associated with the water, gas and electricity supplies. Remember also to check the boiler and telephone, and the television and radio reception.

If you have a moisture meter, test the corners and centre of each wall just above the skirting board; otherwise tap the plaster, feel with a dry hand for damp and coldness, and look out for loose wallpaper or flaking emulsion paint. Check for damp below and around windows, on chimney breasts and at a number of points on the surface of solid floors. In the latter case, tiles or wood blocks may well have

Serious fault in damp-proofing surrounding window and around lintel, causing deep penetration of rainwater. Exact cause may be difficult to determine and expensive to trace and repair

lifted, but in any case observe, touch, smell and prod the concrete screed. Any damp that is evident must be fully tested by a damp-proofing specialist, but try to distinguish between damp and condensation (see Chapter 4).

Test the security of windows and doors. Substantial double locks and bolts on external doors, locks on internal doors operated from the hall, locks on all windows, spyglass in the front door, all-round external lights operated from inside and, of course, the alarm, if one is fitted. Ask the vendor later for a demonstration of how it operates.

On the central heating, observe the condition of each radiator and valve, and on the boiler itself note the age, type and condition and whether there are signs of leakage. Later ask the vendor to demonstrate how to operate the controls for domestic hot water and heating.

Inspect and open all kitchen units and try to glimpse the wall surfaces that they cover for signs of damp. Sketch and list the fittings and equipment, and check with the vendor that they are included in the sale. If equipment or fittings are being removed, ask the vendor how the service connection will be left. Insist, through your solicitor, that electric wiring is left in a safe condition, and that all gas connections are plugged and valved off, as also with water and waste pipes for dishwashers and washing machines.

Before leaving the ground floor, make your notes and sketches and set out the approximate costs of making good the defects and of any necessary alterations.

Cellars

Cellars are notorious for damp, and for wet and dry rot, because often they have little or no ventilation. All timber MUST be treated with preservative. Damp is acceptable so long as the cellar is not in use and so long as it does not rise above the ground floor dpc. If timbers have not already been treated you must call in a wood treatment specialist for a report.

If it looks wrong, it is! Joints are non-existent – the whole floor is relying on a single upright prop which has no restraints

EXTERNAL INSPECTION

Garages and Sheds

Garages and sheds must be surveyed inside and out, as for the main building. Garage floors should be at least 100mm (4in) below the level of the ground floor of the house if they are attached, to avoid entry of petrol and oil spillages. The door, walls and ceiling should have a half-hour fire resistance – do they look as if they have? Now check for damp, ventilation, condensation and for cracks in walls where they join the main building. Cracks under 1mm are acceptable, up to 2mm they require minor repair; above that they require further investigation by a builder or structural engineer.

Detailed External House Inspection

Look carefully at each elevation for cracks, damp, bulges or any kind of distress (see Chapter 4). Any evidence of cracking, other than hairline cracks or damp, needs further expert investigation unless the cause is localised, obvious and easily remedied. Tap all woodwork on windows etc, and external rendering. Dig in here and there with your small screwdriver if you are suspicious of any defect. Is the pointing of the brickwork in good condition? Has the building been changed from the original by additions and alterations, and are these cracking away from the main building? Is the dpc visible and unbridged throughout its length? Is it continuous?

Stand back from the house and observe the roof and

Fig 21   If it looks wrong, it *is* wrong

gutters through binoculars. Is the roof sound? Are all the slates and tiles in place? Are the ridge tiles properly pointed, or has the mortar fallen out? Is there any sagging? Do the gutters look sound? Do they run to falls? Do they appear blocked? If any trees overhang the roof, then there will be problems. Look at the chimney stacks, at the pointing and capping. Look at the TV and other aerials, overhead cables (telephone and/or electrical). Are they all sound and well maintained? Mark your plan and make your notes.

If any walls appear to lean, check by going back to the nearest upper window and drop a plumb line down. Again, this is a serious defect and needs checking by a structural engineer.

Are the walls at eaves level all sound, or are they pushing out, or damp? Make your notes and sketches and then continue.

Mains Services

The vendor may be able to point out external electric cable runs, stop-cocks, gas and water runs, drains and manholes – otherwise you will have to look for them; try to ascertain their age and condition (see Chapter 6). Is the water main in new plastic or old lead? Are the stop-cocks accessible and do they turn easily? Are the mains safely buried, and where they enter the building are they protected and firmly held in position? Are they likely to need renewing? Open all stop-cock covers and test the valves. Check all gullies for condition: are they well concreted in, or do they have gaps which cause spillage onto the external walls and founda-tions? Open up the drain manhole covers with your spade and long screwdrivers. Are the manholes clean? What is the condition of the cement benching? Any backing-up of water indicates a blockage, and any standing water indicates a partial blockage or lack of gravity fall. Turn on the kitchen cold tap and watch the water flow through the manholes. Then place a piece of paper in the nearest WC – flush it, and move quickly to the nearest manhole and watch the

Manhole – rough and defective benching – brickwork needs pointing – flow sluggish

paper flow through. It should flow easily, though not too swiftly, through the manholes, without let or hindrance. Is the brickwork in the manholes firm and sound, and is the pointing in good condition?

Distinguish between the rainwater drains and foul drains by flushing toilets and observing the manholes, then by pouring a bucket of water into external rainwater gullies. Are the two systems separate?

The glazed channels in the manholes should be in sound and near-perfect condition, whether old or new. Any problems with drains should be regarded as a major defect and the details passed on to your solicitor. At worst, they may need digging up and replacing if they are broken, blocked or incorrectly installed. Make your sketches and notes before moving on.

FENCES, DRIVES AND VEGETATION

Determine from the deeds, or ask your solicitor, which fences and hedges belong to the house and are the owner's responsibility to maintain. What standards, if any (height and type) are covenanted for in the documents? Are these being kept? Is renewal or maintenance needed now or in the near future? And those that are the neighbours' responsibility – are they being properly maintained? If hedges exist, then are they still alive and well? Do they need attention? Any problems you find you should photograph and pass to your solicitor for resolving.

Trees and Shrubs

Photograph what is there. Do any roots or overhanging branches affect the house? Are they too near for comfort? Are they alive or dead? Might they blow on to the house?

Trees can damage your walls by
(a) falling
(b) pushing
(c) roots removing moisture from the soil

What about the neighbours' trees? Is the soil sandy or clay? Dig up a spadeful here and there (see Chapter 4 for the effect on foundations). Will this affect your desire (or lack of it) for gardening? If there are choice shrubs in the garden, photograph them and check the agent's particulars, and with your solicitor, to see they are all included.

Walk over the drive and all paved areas. Are they in good condition, especially those close to the house? Any hollows or unevenness indicate either that they have been badly laid or have been affected by subsidence. Will you have to spend money on them? If the drive is shared with a neighbour, is this causing a problem or likely to cause a problem?

Check the gates for condition *and* operation.

Finally, are there any signs whatever of flooding, bad soil, bad drainage, bad smells, harassment or annoyance from neighbours? Is the access for your car and your visitors' cars adequate, or is the road and entrance treated as a public car park?

Think, observe, note!

MEASUREMENT OF HOUSE AND BOUNDARIES

Take the external measurements of the house and out-buildings (you will need these for insurance purposes) to give you an idea of the overall size, which you can obtain by multiplying the area by the number of floors. With the plans from the deeds, measure the four boundaries and check the precise alignment of fences and hedges (the centre of a hedge is usually taken as the boundary position, but not always). Any discrepancies should be noted, drawn, photographed, and passed to your solicitor.

REPORT AND NEGOTIATION
Back to the Vendor

Now seek the vendor and ask about any points that have

arisen in your survey. The vendor can often save you a great deal of trouble, providing the truth is told. Ask about the service agreements, boiler controls, defects, flooding, burglar alarm, drains, guarantees, age of equipment, and neighbours. Check what equipment and fittings will be left and what will be removed; ditto garden shrubs, trees, tubs, greenhouses etc. Be pleasant, don't carp, but act like a corkscrew and draw out all the information you can. As soon as you are safely back in your car, write everything down, but don't necessarily believe it all. Take it with a pinch of salt.

Back to the Solicitor

As soon as possible have your photographs developed and make a summary of all the important defects and other points which you are not happy about as a result of your survey. At the side put down a rough guess of the cost that might be involved. Make two or three fair copies.

Next, go to see the local planning officer and the building control officer and ask them if they know of anything that might affect the house, and show them your list. They are usually very, very helpful and will give you far more information than you will find in the 'search' documents. They will tell you of problems in the area, forthcoming planning proposals, tree preservation orders, which of the drains have been taken over by the Council, road and transport problems, pollution, public rights of way, and so on.

Then, if possible, talk to a friendly builder, architect, structural engineer, surveyor or clerk of works about your particular problems and show them drawings and photographs. Note what they say. They may be able to allay some of your fears or draw attention to further investigation needed.

Now, with your survey summary, the notes of your meeting with the planning office and the advice from your friendly builder, return to your solicitor and present him with the facts. Some matters, such as boundaries, will need to be resolved by him with the vendor's solicitors. Some defects may require further investigation by a structural engineer, builder, damp/wood treatment specialist, Gas/ Electricity/Water Board. If so, ask your solicitor to arrange this, for he will need to obtain the permission of the vendor's solicitor first. He probably knows and can recommend the specialists concerned, but insist that you talk to them first and that any reports are addressed to you (though copied to the solicitor).

If you believe that the property has been seriously overpriced, you should instruct your solicitor to obtain an independent valuation, unless you have a mortgage company which has already done this for you.

When the reports and figures come in, you should discuss them with your solicitor and instruct him to negotiate with the vendor's solicitor a reduction in price to take account of the defects, independent valuation and any discrepancies in boundaries/room sizes. Nearly always some compromise can be reached with the vendor, depending on whether it is a buyer's or a seller's market, but at least you will have the satisfaction of knowing that you've been through everything with a fine tooth comb, that you've done the best you possibly can and know what you are letting yourself in for!

In case you are frightened off, may I say that it is unusual for there to be more than three major matters arising from a survey on the average house. The lesson is, don't lose sight of the wood for the trees. A good resolution before you exchange contracts would be to stand back and have a really long look at the wood!

Finally, if you need a builder to carry out a substantial amount of work on your house after you have purchased it, it is worth considering taking out a BEC Insurance Guarantee for the building work: details in Appendix.

8 · The Future

Future legislation · Caveat emptor (buyer beware)

The National Consumer Council (NCC) is pressing for legislation that would make it compulsory for home-sellers to reveal property faults and potential problems to buyers, and make estate agents liable for the accuracy of the details they publish.

If the past is anything to go by, the position will change but little, and the caveat emptor (buyer beware) principle will prevail. The Law Commission committee says that this principle is not good enough; sellers should be under a legal duty to reveal everything they know and ought to know about their property – which would oblige them to carry out a survey before offering it for sale. Property should come under the Trades Description Act and contracts should allow buyers to back out if they discover undeclared defects. Caveat vendor!

Mrs Sally Oppenheimer-Barnes, the NCC chairman, also wants building societies to become liable for unseen defects such as subsidence, which can cost buyers up to £15,000. Buyers, she says, are put off seeking legal redress, and 'why should the consumer carry the can if the expert fails to notice the house is sinking?'

Why indeed! But unless you want to spend your time and money on litigation against surveyors, building societies, estate agents and solicitors, with no guarantee of success in the end, you need to become as competent as you possibly can in carrying out your own surveys, even if it is simply to check that the 'expert' hasn't missed anything. Building construction should not be a closed book, and the industry itself is neither well trained nor well informed, otherwise its reputation would be a good deal better than it is. Until this changes, the onus is on yourself.

There is here a parallel with conveyancing. As the Lord Chancellor opens the way for banks and building societies to carry out conveyancing, perhaps the best people for the job are the prospective buyers themselves.

How does a solicitor or licensed conveyancer check that a house has no quasi-legal, let alone 'building', defects? Answer: by sending printed forms of questions to the seller's solicitor and the local council, which yield no useful information and are often nothing more than a time-wasting ritual. It would be absurd to send a list of questions to the vendor, such as 'please confirm your roof is working properly', 'please confirm there is nothing wrong with your foundations'. And if there is a long-standing feud with the neighbour over the line of the fence or hedge, will the seller declare it?

The questionnaire sent to the local council (the 'search') is inadequate. In the first place, the questions relate only to the actual house and land being conveyed. They will not reveal any plans to demolish the house next door and erect a block of flats in its place. Secondly, the answers will only reveal any proposals for new roads and so on that have actually been placed on the council's register. There may be others still under discussion – I have heard of a purchaser moving into his new house to find a circular on the doormat inviting him to support a protest against the erection of a 150ft BBC television mast within fifty yards of the house. In another case the owner was advised by the local newspaper of an impending traffic improvement, which was to be either a bypass or a road widening. 'What road widening?' 'Why, through the middle of your house!' was the reply.

If you do your own surveying and/or conveyancing you will spend some time at the Council offices checking with the building and planning officials. But would a solicitor?

Would a professional surveyor? For them, time means money.

You, not they, are the judge of the 'built environment'. According to the Concise Oxford Dictionary, to 'build' means to 'construct by putting parts or material together', whilst 'environment' means 'surrounding objects, region or conditions'. The built environment therefore equates to the sum total of all the assembled items which surround us, both natural and man-made.

Nature, too, plays an important part in the creation of man's built surroundings. It provides the seas, mountains and plains, climate, energy, vegetation, animal life and materials, individually or in combination tending to influence the style, type and location of any house or structure.

Will pollution be the next major factor to be considered, and if so, by whom? Gases are offensive, smells are offensive, grit and dust penetrate houses just as surely as toxic vapours and car fumes. Vibration and noise from traffic – trains, cars, aircraft – affect the nervous system and send tremors through the sub-soil under your house. Who is to judge the effect? Will it be you, or will you leave it to the surveyor and the solicitor? Caveat Emptor!

Case law changes have been coming at frequent intervals, particularly those affecting liability for disclosing defects in house construction. Whatever changes may occur, it is for you, the buyer or seller, to protect your interests, and there is no better way than by carrying out your own survey, whether you have a professional/mortgage survey or not.

Useful Addresses

These are some of the names and addresses of organisations able and willing to help. Information is usually free, and enquiries are welcomed.

Building Centre
26 Store Street, London WC1 7BT
Tel 01 637 1022 (technical information and appointments), or 0344 884999 (product enquiries)
The Information Section will provide details of fact sheets and brochures. (There are also Building Centres in Bristol, Glasgow, Manchester and Newcastle.)

Bituminous Roofing Council
PO Box 125, Haywards Heath, West Sussex
Tel 0444 416681
Technical information and advice on problems with flat roofs.

Brick Development Association
Woodside House, Winkfield, Windsor, Berks SL4 2DX
Tel 0344 885651
Advice on a wide range of building matters, plus information sheets, relating to bricks and brickwork.

British Board of Agrément
PO Box 195, Bucknalls Lane, Garston, Watford, Herts WD2 7NG
Tel 0923 670844 or Hotline Information Service 0923 662900
Information on all approved building products.

British Chemical Dampcourse Association
16a Whitchurch Road, Pangbourne, Reading, Berks RG8 7BP
Tel 07357 3799
Can provide details of chemical damp-proof course installers who subscribe to a Code of Practice, plus information sheets (send sae).

British Wood Preserving Association
Premier House, 150 Southampton Row, London WC1B 5AL
Tel 01 837 8217
Advice and fact sheets on all aspects of wood preservation,
plus details of companies specialising in treating timber
in-situ.

Building Employers' Confederation
82 New Cavendish Street, London W1M 8AD
Tel 01 580 5588
BEC members offer an insurance-backed guarantee scheme
for building works costing £500-£40,000 (see page 149 for
details).

Cavity Foam Bureau
PO Box 79, Oldbury, Warley, West Midlands B69 4PW
Tel 021 544 4949
Technical advice on insulation to British Standard 5618, plus
details of installers who are members of the BSI registered
firms scheme.

Cement and Concrete Association
Wexham Springs, Slough, Berks SL3 6PL
Tel 02816 2727
Free catalogue and publications on the use of concrete around
the home.

Federation of Master Builders
Gordon Fisher House, 33 John Street, London WC1N 2BB
Tel 01 242 7583
Details of builder members.

NICEIC (National Inspection Council for Electrical Installation
Contracting)
Vintage House, 36/37 Albert Embankment, London SE1 7UJ
Tel 01 582 7746
Inspects work of electrical contractors, and investigates
complaints. Publishes list of approved contractors.

Royal Institute of British Architects
66 Portland Place, London W1N 4AD
Tel 01 580 5533
Clients' Advisory Service for selecting an architect.

Royal Institution of Chartered Surveyors
12 Great George Street, Parliament Square, London SW1P 3AD
Tel 01 222 7000
Details of members who will advise on all aspects of
surveying work.

Timber Research and Development Association
Chiltern House, Stocking Lane, Hughenden Valley,
High Wycombe, Bucks HP14 4ND
Tel 024024 3091
Advice, data sheets and publications available.

British Standards Institution
2 Park Street, London W1A 2RS
Tel 01 629 9000
Information available includes *Buyers Guide*, free brochure
'As Safe As Houses', and a booklet called 'Playing Safe', price
50p.

Consumers' Association
2 Marylebone Road, London NW1 4DX
Tel 01 935 1606
Chief publication is *Which?* magazine. Legal advice on goods
or services is available through the *Which?* Personal Service
for members.

NHBC (National House-Building Council)
Chiltern Avenue, Amersham, Bucks HP6 5AP
Tel Amersham 4477
Technical queries about NHBC standards dealt with in writing.

CORGI (Confederation for the Registration of Gas Installers)
St Martin's House, 140 Tottenham Court Road, London
W1P 9LN
Tel 01 387 9185
Maintains a Register of Installers of mains gas appliances.

External Wall Insulation Association
PO Box 12, Haslemere, Surrey GU27 3AN
Tel 0428 54011
Technical advice and members' list of manufacturers and
contractors.

Royal Society for the Prevention of Accidents
Cannon House, The Priory, Queensway, Birmingham B4 6DC
Tel: 021 233 2461
Information and leaflets available.

Centre on Environment for the Handicapped
126 Albert Street, London NW1 7NF
Tel 01 482 2247
Provides a specialist information and advisory service on
architecture and design for the handicapped and elderly.

Building Research Establishment
Department of the Environment, Garston, Watford, Herts
WD2 7JR
Research and information on all building subjects.

HMSO Bookshops
49 High Holborn, London; and in Birmingham, Bristol,
Manchester, Belfast and Edinburgh
Free list of titles, *Architecture and Building* in subject categories.

Local Gas, Electricity and Water Boards.

Institution of Structural Engineers
11 Upper Belgrave Street, London W1N 4AD
Tel 01 235 4535
Advisory service on selection of structural engineers.

Appendix

The BEC Guarantee Scheme for Building Contracts

The Building Employers' Confederation Building Trust wants people to make use of its revolutionary guarantee scheme, designed to take the worry out of small building contracts by guaranteeing that whatever happens to the builder, contracted work will be completed to a proper standard. Of course, builders give guarantees, and in some cases they may not be worth the paper they are written on, but behind the BEC scheme is a substantial insurance company and the considerable weight of the BEC itself, which speaks with a much more authoritative voice than that of the lone home-owner.

The BEC Guarantee Scheme was launched in 1984 after three years of study and development in conjunction with the Office of Fair Trading. The Guarantee covers work done by its members. In return for a premium of one per cent (minimum £20) on the value of the contract, the home owner gets the following benefits:

* Disputes that cannot be settled between client and builder are referred to a conciliator and, if that does not produce a solution, to an arbitrator. (There is a £25 returnable deposit to deter frivolous complainers at the conciliation stage and £50 at arbitration. In any event, neither party will be asked to pay more than £250 of the actual arbitration costs.)

* Work, goods and materials are covered by full insurance against all risk of damage.

* Should the builder not carry out his contract satis-factorily, the BEC steps in and ensures that work is completed and any defects remedied.

* For six months after the completion of the contract, any work which turns out not to have been done properly will be put right.

* For two years after completion of the contract, any structural defect in the foundations or load-bearing part of a roof, floor or wall which is the fault of the member builder who carried out the initial work, will be put right.

* Even more importantly, work left undone, or contracts left unfinished, because the member builder has gone out of business, will be completed by another member of the Confederation.

There is an upper limit on the value of compensation work that can be carried out under the Guarantee of £6,500 – which includes any professional fees required and any VAT. If the maximum compensation seems small, it is worth remembering that the average size of the 7,672 contracts so far covered by the scheme has been just under £8,000, so it is highly unlikely that any client of a Confederation member has found him or herself out of pocket as a result of any member's behaviour. There is a limit on the size of contract that can be covered by the Guarantee. If you employ the builder directly you can use the scheme on contracts from £500 to £40,000 in size. If an architect or other professional acts on your behalf to supervise the contract, then the better value you are likely to get is reflected in a higher upper limit of £50,000. Both figures are exclusive of VAT.

The BEC Guarantee covers virtually all domestic building works likely to be required within the price ranges speci-fied. There are, however, some exclusions. Swimming pools are not included because faults, when they do arise, can be highly expensive to put right. To include them would be to push the premium up to unacceptable heights. Solar heating is excluded for the same reason. New roofing is included provided the whole roof is renewed. Roof repairs are often hard to control and are therefore not included. It is well known in the building trade that if a fault is found in one part of a roof dozens more will be found elsewhere once remedial work is begun. Landscaping is not strictly building work, and is not included in the guarantee.

There are a few other small rules. Work must be carried out under either the BEC's standard form of contract or the Joint Contracts Tribunal's Agreement for Minor Building Works. These contracts simply lay out the terms of the agreement with the builder in a formalised way so that disagreements about what was agreed are kept to a minimum.

Your contract with the BEC Building Trust must be registered before work begins. Your builder is responsible for registering the work under the guarantee, but details may be obtained by writing to BEC Building Trust Ltd, Medway House, London Road, Maidstone, Kent ME16 0DU. Most BEC members also have copies of the literature outlining the scheme. If you do not know a member builder, the BEC Building Trust will supply a list of members in your district.

Index

Plumbing, *see* Water services
Porches, 49, 56, 73, 121
Purlins, *see* Roofs, structure

Rafters, *see* Roofs, structure
Rainwater pipes, *see* Drains
Rights of way, *see* Access
Roofs, 32, 67–75, 85, 87, 120,
    133; coverings, 44, 45, 67, 87,
    134; damp, 43; downpipes,
    gullies, gutters, *see* Drains;
    flat roofs, 73, 145; insulation,
    21, 42, 43, 73, 126; leaks, 53;
    structure, 21, 29, 55, 57, 67, 87,
    122, 123–7, *see also* Structural
    defects
Rot, *see* Dry rot; Wet rot
Royal Institution of Chartered
    Surveyors (RICS), 18, 23, 24,
    29, 146

Septic tanks, *see* Drains
Sewers, *see* Drains
Silicone injection, *see* Damp
    treatment
Soakaways, *see* Drains
Solid fuel, *see* Heating
Staircases, 56, 60, 85, 129
Structural defects, 19, 29, 31,
    34, 53–83, 123–5, 128, 132,
    134, 139; *see also* Foundations;
    Roofs; Walls
Structural engineers, 14, 24, 79,
    81, 90, 96, 128, 132, 134, 139,
    140, 148
Survey documents, 119, 120,
    139
Survey report, 27, 138–40
Survey valuations, 22, 23, 140

Telephones, 116, 117, 121, 129,
    134

Terraced houses, 50, 85–8, 126;
    see also Flats
Timber, 21, 55, 147; *see also*
    Woodwork
Timber frame houses, 87–98
Trees, 55, 77, 78, 79, 101, 121,
    134, 136, 137, 138, 139
TV and radio, 121, 129, 134

Underpinning, 79, 80

Ventilation, 57, 58, 60, 63, 70,
    71, 73, 94, 107, 109, 126, 128,
    131, 132

Walls; cavities and ties, 55, 60,
    62, 76, 80–3; cavity insulation,
    81–4, 146; cracks and bulges,
    31, 43, 44, 53, 77, 78–83, 123,
    124, 128, 131, 132, 133, 134,
    137; *see also* Flats and party
    walls; Foundations; Roofs;
    Terraced houses
Water services and plumbing,
    59, 60, 104–14, 121, 123, 124,
    129, 134
Water storage tanks, 43, 73, 104,
    105, 111–3, 126, 127
Wet rot, 21, 28, 33, 53, 56, 58–
    60, 67, 123–7, 129; *see also* Dry
    rot
Windows, 28, 32, 53, 56, 69, 73,
    74, 129, 133
Wood treatment, 33, 58–60, 131,
    140, 146
Woodwork, 55, 58, 59, 127, 133;
    see also Timber
Woodworm, 21, 42, 56, 58–60,
    67, 73, 126, 127, 129; *see also*
    Deathwatch beetle